Syd Dernley was born in Mansfield Woodhouse, Notts., in 1920. At the age of fifteen he left grammar school to become a stores boy at the local colliery, and he stayed at the pit for the next thirty years.

As a boy, his imagination was fired by Edgar Wallace's crime stories and, aged only twelve, he decided that he wanted to be a hangman. That ambition was realized in 1949. Over the next four years he helped to hang more than twenty murderers.

Syd Dernley is now retired and lives in Mansfield with his wife Joyce. He is treasurer of his local Conservative Club.

David Newman began his career as a print journalist, but switched to broadcasting in 1971. After four years working in BBC local radio, he joined Radio Trent, the commercial station in Nottingham, where he is now the Regional News Editor.

He began working with Syd Dernley on this book after a radio programme about capital punishment at the time of a parliamentary debate on the subject. He lives with his wife Diana in Barton-upon-Humber.

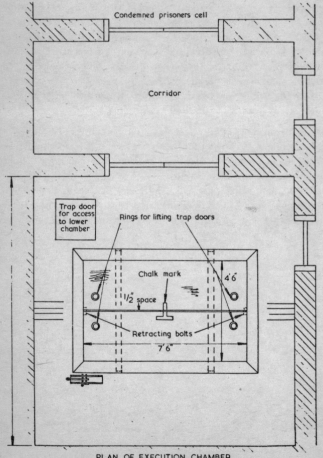

PLAN OF EXECUTION CHAMBER

Syd Dernley with David Newman

THE HANGMAN'S TALE

Memoirs of a Public Executioner

PAN BOOKS
London, Sydney and Auckland

First published in Great Britain 1989 by Robert Hale Limited
This edition published 1990 by Pan Books Limited,
Cavaye Place, London SW10 9PG

1 3 5 7 9 8 6 4 2

© Syd Dernley and David Newman 1989
ISBN 0 330 31633 8

Printed in England by Clays Ltd, St Ives plc

Contents

List of Illustrations		7
Acknowledgements		9
Introduction		11
1	The Journey	13
2	Application	25
3	The Mysteries	32
4	The Real Thing	48
5	The Innocent Man	70
6	'You Will Hang by the Neck …'	83
7	Bungling Bank Robbers	93
8	The News Gets Out	105
9	'I Want to Hang'	116
10	A Rotten Job	127
11	Bribery!	142
12	Two Days, Three Hangings	151
13	One for the Record Books	163
14	Lovers, an Invitation to a New Year's Party, and More Innocent Men	174
15	The Sack?	185
16	Conclusions	193
Index		203

Illustrations

Between pp. 96 and 97

1 Syd Dernley with Joyce Harston at the time of their engagement
2 Hangmen and friends after an execution at Shrewsbury
3 The rules of office
4 Edward Devlin, the hard man who crumbled in the condemned cell
5 On 27th February 1952, Alfred Burns was hanged in Liverpool
6 A specially commissioned Christmas card from one of Syd Dernley's fans
7 The gallows – Syd made a miniature model
8 The Hull murderer James Inglis arriving at court
9 The official letter detailing the arrangements of the execution of Timothy Evans
10 Evans arriving back in London with detectives
11 The equipment: rope, leg-strap, arm-strap and linen hood
12 Syd Dernley today, now retired and living in Mansfield
13 For many years, Syd had the only privately owned gallows in the country
14 Syd Dernley and David Newman discuss capital punishment on Radio Trent

PICTURE CREDITS

Geoff Peabody Associates, Nottingham: 7, 11, 12, 14; *Hull Daily Mail*: 8; Syndication International: 10.

It has not been possible to trace the copyright holders of pictures 4 and 5, though their work appeared in the *Sunday Express* on 24 January 1971. The photographers should contact the publishers with any query on the matter.

The back jacket photograph shows Syd Dernley today (*courtesy of Geoff Peabody Associates, Nottingham*).

Acknowledgments

We have been helped by many people during the writing of this book and we would like to record our grateful thanks to them:

To journalists Jane Woodall, Steve Kyte and Philip Hopkins who helped with research into particular cases.

To Martin Brandon-Bravo, Member of Parliament for Nottingham South, and Richard Ottoway, Member of Parliament for Nottingham North 1983-87, for assistance with certain legal problems.

To Diana Newman, Joan Barlow and Angela Walker who transcribed tapes of our endless conversations and typed and re-typed the manuscript.

Finally a special word for the librarians in reference sections and local history departments up and down the country, from Durham to Bristol. For the most part we did not know their names and they did not know what we were about but they were unfailingly helpful and always prepared to enter the dustiest parts of their domains to find the information we needed.

Introduction

The first hanging was shattering. As a trainee executioner I was there to watch. I did not have to do anything except stay on my feet and keep my breakfast down.

The execution was timed for nine o'clock on the morning of Thursday, 29 March 1949, at Winson Green Prison in Birmingham. James Farrell, the Hollybush Murderer, was to be hanged by England's chief executioner Albert Pierrepoint and his assistant Harry Kirk. Farrell had raped a fourteen-year-old schoolgirl and then strangled her; the body was then dumped in hollybushes at a beauty spot. In spite of the disgusting nature of the crime, it would have been a completely unremarkable execution but for Farrell's age; his nineteenth birthday had occurred in the condemned cell just three days before he was to die. He would be the youngest man to be hanged in Britain for thirty years.

At two minutes to nine o'clock, another trainee, Harry Allen, and myself were standing outside the door of the execution chamber, which was located at first-landing level in a wing of the prison. A few yards down the corridor Pierrepoint and Kirk were in position at the door of the condemned cell. At the very instant that nine o'clock struck, the executioners were given a signal and they darted into the condemned cell.

As they disappeared, we were taken directly into the execution chamber. The room was quite small, only about fourteen feet square, with plain brick walls painted white. High on the opposite wall was the only window, which was barred and had netting on the inside. The floor was wooden, and taking up a large part of it were the great trapdoors. For the rest, there was just a pair of parallel beams running across the cell over the centre of the trap, at a height of eight or ten feet, and the rope was hanging down from them; the slack collected in a series of loops, fastened with thread, so that the noose was motionless at head height.

Harry and I were pushed into position against a wall. The governor of the prison, the under-sheriff and other prison officials, were already waiting. Some of them looked grey and drawn; they were all staring at a pair of yellow double doors in the wall to the right. They led to the condemned cell and had already been flung wide open.

We were in the chamber for only a few seconds when the execution started. Through the yellow doors came Pierrepoint: a smallish man, only about 5 feet 6 inches tall, neatly dressed in a blue lounge suit. Out of the breast pocket of his jacket flopped what looked for all the world like a foppishly worn handkerchief, but was in fact the hood to go over the head of the condemned man.

Farrell, arms already strapped behind his back, followed a pace behind Pierrepoint. All I could see of him was a big bush of blond hair and the most terrified eyes I had ever seen in my life. Kirk was following but not having to push or urge the condemned man on.

Pierrepoint walked straight across the trapdoor, turned, and stopped Farrell in the middle of the trap by stretching out both his arms and lightly resting them on the man's shoulders. In a flash the hood was out of Pierrepoint's pocket and over Farrell's head. Kirk was down behind, putting a strap round the ankles. Pierrepoint flicked the noose over the hooded head and leant over to tap Kirk on the shoulder; he threw himself off the trap-door as Pierrepoint went to the left and pushed over the lever. The whole floor seemed to collapse; Farrell plunged downwards and there was an enormous boom which must have been heard over half the prison as those massive doors crashed against the walls of the pit. It was over.

In the quiet which followed, I heard an official say, 'Eight seconds. Well done!'

EIGHT SECONDS!

I was stunned by the speed of it ... after the trial ... after sentence by a judge wearing a black cap ... after the weeks of waiting in the condemned cell, never left alone day or night ... James Farrell, rapist and killer, had been in the company of the executioners for exactly eight seconds! That was from the moment Pierrepoint and Kirk entered the condemned cell until the moment he was hanging dead on the end of the rope ... EIGHT SECONDS!

1 The Journey

I decided to become a hangman when I was eleven years old. It all started when I was browsing along the shelves of the small local library at Mansfield Woodhouse in Nottinghamshire and, by chance, picked up a book by Edgar Wallace. In the early years of the century, newspapermen were allowed to witness executions; Wallace had seen a couple of hangings and when he later turned his hand to writing crime thrillers, he made good use of the experience. I was fascinated by the tension and drama of the preparations for the execution and when I closed the covers of the book, I found myself thinking that I could do that … I could be an executioner.

At the outset, I should make it clear that I never saw myself as an avenger with some sort of mission, and I must say that if the hand of God ever moved anyone to become a hangman – and several have claimed that it did – then it was not so in my case.

I did not have a strange family background either. The Dernley family is quite free of blame; they had never produced anyone even remotely involved in the maintenance of law and order before and would no doubt have been shattered to realize that they would, one day, produce a hangman!

The Dernleys were country folk who, for generations, served on the great aristocratic estates in Sherwood Forest. My father William started work as a young lad on the lands of the Duke of Portland at Welbeck Abbey, as his father had before him, and his father before him. Dad eventually left to strike out on his own, first as a market gardener and then as a grocer, but he was forced to take a secure job, as an insurance agent, just before I was born on 29th December 1920.

My life would probably have turned out quite differently had he stayed with the Duke at Welbeck; I would, likely as not, have become a forester or gamekeeper on the estate. Certainly he would have been happier because neither the passing years nor the experience of being his own boss made any difference; he was a Duke's man to the end of his life. It sounds strange today, but he worshipped the Duke and Duchess, even though Their Graces scarcely spoke more than a few words to him during all the time that he worked for them.

As it was, he never entirely severed his links with the estate. We still had relatives working there and he made sure that we rarely missed the annual Welbeck Gala, a great local event. One of my earliest memories is of being taken, as a young boy of four or five, to the gala. At a distance we saw the Duke and Duchess strolling through the crowds and Dad showed me, for the first time, the strange wonders which made Welbeck Abbey one of the most famous country houses in Europe.

Incredible underground constructions had been carried out at the Abbey on the orders of the Duke's father, the Fifth Duke, more commonly known as the Mad Duke. He was a mysterious man who was rumoured to be appallingly badly disfigured; I say rumoured, because he was a recluse and never allowed anyone to look at him. My father told me that in all the years that he worked on the estate – and he started only a few years after the Mad Duke's death in 1879 – he never met anyone who had actually seen his face. The handful of older estate workers who had been in brief contact with him could report only that a coach, with all but one of its blinds drawn down, had stopped near them and they had been addressed by a shadowy figure speaking from the dark interior.

Inevitably there was endless and fantastic rumour, the most favoured story being that syphilis had caused hideous damage and the Duke could not bear anyone to look upon his monstrous appearance. Whatever the truth of the matter, such a strange personality, having almost unlimited wealth at its disposal, was likely to have unexpected results – and it did. For years the Mad Duke had thousands of people employed in digging underground tunnels which ran all over the estate, below the forest floor. They were enormous, big enough to take a coach and four, so that the Duke could travel about, unseen.

It did not stop there. Entire suites of rooms were constructed underground at the Abbey, including an immense ballroom which was said to be the largest room in a private house in England. Years later, thinking back to tales of the Mad Duke told around a blazing fire of a winter's evening, it struck me as rather strange that a hideously disfigured man, who could not bear anyone to look at him, should want the biggest ballroom in England!

Nevertheless, ballroom and tunnels certainly did exist. That afternoon at the gala, Dad and I slipped away from the crowds, went down a narrow flight of steps, and emerged into one of the main underground passageways. It seemed huge; the walls were stone, as was the roof which arched over our heads. We stood on the cobbled roadway, along which the Mad Duke's coach had thundered; the tunnel stretched out of sight into the gloom in both directions.

During the day, light filtered into the tunnels through ventilators, glass things about a yard across, which stuck up above the floor of the forest. Dad said that at night the tunnels were lit by gas lamps high on the walls. When he was a boy, one of his jobs on many an evening had been to ride along the tunnels lighting the lamps, standing on the back of a pony like a trick rider in a circus to reach high enough. I listened, open-mouthed, and then he led the way through a largish opening in the side of the tunnel and we were standing in the small underground stable where the ponies had been kept all those years ago. Now they were clean and gloomy, and obviously long unused.

A few moments later we headed back for the sunshine and the gala but by a new and even more wonderful route. We took a rough, narrow little passageway and emerged into the peach house. I had never even seen a peach and here were trees just laden with them.

'Are they nice to eat?' I asked, hopefully.

'Aye, I expect so,' Dad replied.

'Can I have one?' I asked.

'No you can't! They belong to the Duke,' he replied. And that, so far as he was concerned, was that.

I was fascinated by the tunnels and after that first time we always explored them when we went to the gala. In later years I saw the underground ballroom where there had been magnificent banquets and dances attended by royalty and the cream of society. Dad told me he had been too young to wait at table but he had been allowed to peep round the door at the scene. We stood at the very same doorway, looking into the cold, dark room, and I tried to imagine what it must have been like, blazing with light and filled with all those important lords and ladies.

By comparison with all this, the Dernley family lifestyle was somewhat modest! Soon after I was born, Mam and Dad had been given a new three-bedroomed council house in Mansfield Woodhouse. When we moved in, so did Mam's spinster sister Violet, whose chap had been killed in the First World War, and their father, Grandad Reuben Thompson; I shared my bedroom with him until I was twelve years old.

We were, by most standards, fairly poor; we ate well enough but there was never much money about. As a boy, I was never particularly conscious of it simply because everyone else who lived around us was in pretty much the same state. My pocket money was just tuppence a week, but I was as well off as Reg Lilliman, who lived next door, and even a ha'penny bought a big bag of aniseed balls at Mr Owen's corner shop. The toffs seemed to be able to buy a Mars Bar every day; I was not often affected by envy of such unimaginable riches, although there were exceptional circumstances from time to time.

One of the boys who lived nearby, whose parents had more money than mine, had been bought a toy aeroplane. No-one would believe just how much I coveted that little wooden bi-plane; I lusted after it for months, without even the slightest hope that my parents would ever buy me one. When I suggested a swap, all he was interested in was my tortoise, the one thing in all the world that I would not part with, even for the beloved plane. Negotiations were in a state of deadlock when, in the middle of summer, the tortoise died.

I blush to say that shock and grief for the demise of my pet were rapidly followed by the realization that as the tortoise had retreated into its shell to die, it was still an asset. I put it into a box of straw and re-opened talks that very day. When the aircraft owner said the tortoise did not seem to be doing much, I told him that it had gone into hibernation. The deal went through but, with the aeroplane at last in my hands, I became dangerously expansive. 'Keep it warm', I told him, 'and it'll come to life in the spring.'

That advice was my undoing! He took it home and put it in the airing cupboard. It was not many days before a highly dissatisfied customer was standing on my doorstep, demanding the return of his aeroplane. 'Me Mam says that tortoise is stinking the house out! She says its dead and I've got to bury it!'

'It'll come to life in the spring!' I protested.

This time, however, he was not to be convinced. I had to relinquish my ownership of the aeroplane, but the days of possession had cooled my jealousy and the long-dead tortoise finally got a decent burial.

At school I did quite well, at least to begin with, and I was one of only three boys from my year at the York Street Juniors to pass the scholarship and go to the famous Brunts Grammar School. No doubt, if that early promise had been maintained I would have ended up working in a bank or an office, in a respectable job where they would not have been happy for me to slip off for a couple of days, every now and then, to hang some murderer. What actually happened was that I peaked in the first year at Brunts, when I achieved twenty-fourth place out of thirty-five, and I slid ever nearer the bottom of the class after that. I do not believe I was dim; if that had been the case I think my teachers and my parents would have given me a slightly easier time than they did. They said I was living in another world and they were right; I was living in a world of books – a world of murders and famous detectives and trials … and executions.

In the end neither I nor the schoolmasters felt any great sense of loss when we parted company just before my sixteenth birthday. Times in the Dernley household had become ever harder as the thirties wore on, the insurance business became just about impossible and eventually Dad was finished. He was out of work for a long time and when he did finally get another job it was only as a groundsman. After the years of struggling, it came as no surprise when he said that he could not afford to keep me at school any longer and it would be best if I started work. Brunts broke up for Christmas and I never went back.

I reported for duty at Sherwood Colliery on 1st January. I was taken on as a stores lad; my father knew Eric Crooks who was in charge there. Everything anyone could want at the pit was in our building, from the colliers' pickaxe handles to the oil in their lamps. We also kept all the parts needed for the machinery, the winding engines above ground and the conveyors and cutters below. My job was to lug the stores up the stairs and the ladders in the stores when they arrived, back down the same ladders and the same stairs when they were wanted. Nuts and bolts arrived in hundredweight bags, fifty bags at a time, once a month. It was not long before I could dispense with the bodybuilding weights I had been using to develop my muscles. Having said that, I could not have any illusions about it being a tough job; all I had to do was look at the hands of any collier who came to get a shovel – battered and scarred and misshapen by great calluses to know when I was well off. I quickly decided that I would not work underground for all the tea in China.

I was still reading all the crime books I could lay my hands on and, now that I was earning some money, I even started my own collection. I also took up shooting and joined a gun club at Mansfield, where it soon became apparent that here I had found something at which I could really excel. As time passed I became a pretty handy shot, handy enough, I thought, to be of use when the war came along. By this time I had left the stores and trained as a welder. Mining was a reserved occupation, so I did not have to join up, but I thought about it hard and, early in 1940, I came to the conclusion that I should join the air force, preferably on bombers and preferably as a gunner.

This was a major crossroads in my life. Had I joined up, or had my ambition ever been sympathetically heard out, I doubt the hangman would ever have emerged. Even if I had survived the war – and I realize that on bombers that is a big if – I would no doubt have been happy to settle for a normal, humdrum life later. It was not to be. There was no sympathetic hearing; I got a bollocking. About two minutes was all it took for the idea of joining up to be kicked out of me, and I remember each of those terrible, humilating minutes as if they had just occurred.

I had to see my boss, the pit engineer Bernard Eddershaw. He was working on some papers at his desk when I entered his office.

'Yes, Dernley?' he said, looking up.

'I've been thinking about joining up, Mr Eddershaw,' I told him.

There was no reaction. Nothing. It was almost as if he had not heard what I said.

'I've been thinking about joining up,' I repeated. 'I want to go into the air force.'

A look of contempt swept across his face but for several seconds more he still did not say anything. Then, when his words did come, the tone was icy.

'Yes, you can join the air force, Dernley – but there'll be no job for you here when you come back.'

I was stunned. I had not expected this reaction at all and I stood there, shocked and not knowing what to say. Eventually I stammered out something about thinking again and fled from Eddershaw's office, my face burning with humiliation and embarrassment.

I was still shaken that evening when I told them at home about that brief and brutal interview, but there was no sympathy in this quarter either.

'Better stop at the pit then,' said my father. And he immediately disappeared behind his paper again.

I bottled out, and my misery was complete a few days later when Eddershaw summoned me to his office. He found out that I was staying on, and promptly put me on nights; an arrangement which was to last for the duration of the conflict.

It was not the sort of war to be proud of, particularly when the Brunts School magazine carried news that one or other of the lads who had sat in class with me a few years before, had been killed in action.

For a time, the excitement and adventure that I craved came secretly – and disreputably – in the glades of Sherwood Forest. The woodland was by this time only a small fragment of the enormous forest which had sheltered Robin Hood and the outlaws in medieval times, but it still covered at least part of central Nottinghamshire. Most of it was included in three great aristocratic estates: Welbeck, Clumber Park and Thoresby. In one respect the great estates were identical: they were all teeming with pheasants and partridges, wild duck and other water fowl; they even had deer. It would have been a poacher's paradise had it not been for the army of gamekeepers, gatekeepers and estate workers whose job, to a greater or lesser extent, was to make sure that likely lads with a bit of nerve and tastes above their station did not get their hands on Their Lordship's plump pheasants.

My partner in crime was a chap called Derek Cutbush. He could not shoot but he had a car and worked in the forest, cutting down trees; he knew the woodland well. He approached me in a pub and we were soon clinking our glasses to 'a pheasant or two … and perhaps something bigger'.

It was an unholy and highly successful alliance and we got

away with it for months. We never even saw a keeper as pheasants, partridges, rabbits and sometimes, after a particularly good shot, a hare, followed each other into the pot. Derek turned out to be a real Mr Fixit. Despite petrol rationing, he always seemed to manage a full tank for our poaching trips, and when ammunition became more difficult to get, he knew somebody who knew somebody and we never ran short of that either. On one occasion he even turned up with a box of army tracer bullets. They were great for shooting in windy conditions because you could see where they were going – a red streak – and adjust accordingly.

It was all so easy that we started to get cocky and began to do things which, a few months earlier, we would have thought were mad. Matters came to a head one day when we were cruising through the forest as dusk was falling. I was loading the gun, and in the poor light I did not notice the tracer shell which had got mixed in with the other ammunition. Derek drove into the estate past a keeper's lodge (that's how casual we were getting). A bare hundred yards after the cottage, he braked and said, 'Behind!'

He had spotted a pheasant on the edge of the wood as we passed it and the bird was now trotting across the track. Without a thought I was out of the car and bringing the gun to bear, I squeezed the trigger – and all hell broke loose!

First there was a damn great crack as the gun fired; the silencer did not work on the tracers, which were lighter than normal ammo. We saw the bullet streak straight through the pheasant, which was knocked up in the air, then the bullet ricocheted off a stone and headed for the roof of the lodge, where there was another great crack as it hit the chimney-pot.

'Christ, that's buggered it!' said Derek, awestruck.

I felt rooted to the spot.

'Come on Syd!' he urged. 'Let's get going!'

Even as we started moving towards the car, we could hear the uproar at the lodge. Doors were banging and there were voices bawling and shouting.

With the quick way off the estate barred, we roared off into the forest, but only a couple of minutes later Derek announced, 'We've got company!'

I looked back and there were headlights behind us. Derek was driving for his life and the car was fair flying along the estate road but he was keeping his lights switched off and they were gaining on us.

'We'll lose them at the church,' Derek told me, as I clung on for dear life. The car was bouncing all over the place in what was now almost complete darkness.

The spot he was aiming for was a church in the middle of Clumber Park which was ringed with estate roads going off in all directions. If we could reach that we had a pretty good chance of throwing our pursuers off the trail. At the moment it seemed unlikely that we would make it. 'They're still gaining on us!' I told him.

It was unnecessary advice. They were now so close behind us that on the straight parts of the road their headlamps were lighting up the inside of our car.

'I daren't go any faster without lights,' he told me, 'and if I put 'em on, he'll see where we turn off.'

As we hit the circle round the church we were no more than a few hundred yards ahead of them. Derek screeched round and then hurtled off along a new road.

Hardly daring to breathe, I watched the road behind us … nothing. 'I think we've shaken them off,' I said.

It was with a great feeling of relief that we emerged, a few minutes later, on one of the main roads through the forest and a short distance from the Normanton Inn.

'Fancy a pint?' laughed Derek.

'By God, I'm ready for one!' I agreed.

Standing at the bar in the taproom, we drank to our narrow escape. I had managed just one mouthful when a commotion broke out across the bar in the best room. The door burst open and in strode a great, tall chap – Carey the head keeper – and two of his henchmen! He looked around and then spotted us through in the taproom. 'Them's the buggers!' he shouted and they charged for the door.

We didn't stop to argue or find out how they knew we were the buggers. We fled!

The chase started again, but this time, with our lights on, we soon lost them.

We eased up on the trips to the woods after that. It was a decision which would soon have been forced on us anyway. The army moved into the forest and started storing munitions there. Soon the area was crawling with thousands of soldiers and guards. They also took over the rifle club range and the club closed down for the duration of the war, making it almost impossible to get ammunition. Derek went into the army, where he proved less adept at dodging Germans than gamekeepers, and ended up as a prisoner.

Not long afterwards I got married. It was a fairly remarkable courtship, considering that I was working permanently on nights. In fact, little short of miraculous considering that she was working days for her parents, who ran the biggest newsagents in Mansfield Woodhouse, and evenings at the Tivoli, the local cinema.

Joyce was small and pretty, with black hair and rosy cheeks. I thought she was smashing, although it took me long enough to do anything about it. I had never been out with a girl before and I had never been one for the smooth patter, but somehow we started to smile at each other as we passed early in the morning, she on her way to deliver newspapers and me on my way home from the pit.

One day she said to me, 'Wish me many happy returns ... it's my birthday.'

'Many happy returns', I said, 'and you'd better wish *me* happy birthday – it's my birthday too!'

'I don't believe you,' she said incredulously. 'How old are you?'

'Twenty,' I replied.

'You're pulling my leg!' she laughed. 'I'm twenty!'

She took some convincing but we really were born on the very same day. More importantly, it broke the ice and I asked her for a date.

We were married at St Edmund's Church at Mansfield Woodhouse on 27th October 1943. Like most other weddings in those war years, it was small and involved only close family. Fashion and necessity dictated against the flash and extravagant, and Joyce's father was not the man to buck a trend like that. Less than a dozen people were invited back to the shop for a sandwich, and before the reception was over, the shop had re-opened for business. He closed for just an hour.

After the honeymoon in Scarborough, we returned to live with my parents for five months, but then we were allocated a small colliery house which cost us six shillings a week in rent. We had free coal and cheap electricity from the colliery power house, and we were as snug as could be. The months and then the years rolled by. The war ended, I finally came off nights, life settled into a quiet routine and I began to think again about that long-held ambition: to become a hangman.

For a time I did nothing about the idea, and I got all the excitement I could handle when I was persuaded to go poaching again. I had a new partner and this time things were to be different. Derek and I had been content with the odd pheasant or two, for our own pots, but to my new associate it was business. He had customers who had to be supplied!

Lofty had served in the SAS during the war and had been involved in raids on Greece. He was completely nerveless and he was also a villain. Among other things he had been convicted of poaching and was banned from having a fire-arm – which is why he needed me.

The woods were teeming with game after the war and it was almost too easy, or it would have been had Lofty not possessed a suicidal love of danger and excitement. A typical example of his peculiar madness came one afternoon when we had been in operation on the Welbeck Estate. We had enjoyed a brilliantly successful trip and bagged nine or ten birds. It was not enough; on the way home he drove right past the front of the Abbey. I was terrified; Lofty went past waving to the people inside!

I soon learned that much as you might like a rogue like Lofty, you should never trust one. Even his paying customers were not safe from his trickery. There was one incident which occurred in Clumber Park just before Christmas when we came across a badly injured swan. It had flown into some telegraph wires and was obviously in great pain.

'I'll put it out of its misery,' I told Lofty, and quickly despatched it.

He walked over to have a look and then, to my astonishment, picked it up and put it in the car.

'What on earth are you doing?' I asked.

He winked. 'Never you mind. I take it you don't want it?'

I certainly had no use for a dead swan, and after I had dropped him off that afternoon I thought no more about it. Not, that is, until a few weeks after Christmas when we found ourselves having a drink at the Young Vanish Inn at Glapwell. I knew that the landlord was one of Lofty's customers, and we always had a friendly welcome when we dropped in.

I was halfway through a pint when Lofty turned to me with a grin and asked, 'You remember that swan we got?'

I nodded.

'Did I tell you I sold it?' he asked, knowing perfectly well that he had not told me.

'How the hell did you manage that?' I asked. 'Who would want a swan?'

'Sold it to a chap for thirty bob ... told him it was a goose!' he said.

I burst out laughing. He really was the end! 'Who was the mug?' I finally managed to ask.

Lofty laughed and nodded along the bar to where the landlord was pulling a pint. 'Him!'

A few minutes later the landlord came over and stood with us for a chat. With an absolutely straight face, Lofty asked casually, 'Oh, by the way, how was that goose I got for you?'

'It wasn't bad', replied the landlord, 'except do you know, it tasted a bit fishy.'

'Fishy!' exclaimed Lofty in mock surprise. 'How strange!'

'Yes, weird, really,' said the landlord. 'It wasn't bad though.'

I studied my pint, held my breath and tried to stop myself exploding with laughter. How I kept a straight face I will never know, and I was rarely so pleased to get out of a pub in my life.

Eventually, despite Lofty's mad antics, the poaching began to lose its excitement, and I finally decided to do something about my great ambititon.

By this time I had a very good collection of books on crime and capital punishment. I often went to auctions and sometimes bought a whole box of books for just one volume. I also advertised in *Exchange & Mart*, and that led to a contact with a chap in Bradford who had a lot of material on James Berry, the Yorkshireman who was the chief executioner in the latter years of the nineteenth century. I bought the book version of Berry's autobiography, and a number of copies of a Yorkshire paper in which Berry's life had been serialized.

It was his story which crystallized my thoughts about becoming a hangman. It was not that I wanted to kill people, but it was the story of travel and adventure, of seeing notorious criminals and meeting famous detectives. The craft would take me into the world I had been reading about for so long.

2 Application

Deciding to be an executioner was one thing but, as I was soon to find out, actually becoming one was not such a simple matter. For a start, vacancies were never advertised. I found out later that there were always more than enough people offering their services and a really brutal murder brought applications flooding in. I did not have a clue about how to apply, so I did what any loyal reader of the *News of the World* with a problem would do: I wrote to the paper's advice column, the John Hilton Bureau.

My letter to the Bureau was short, just a couple of lines: 'Dear Sir, I want to become a hangman. Can you tell me how I go about applying for the job?'

At the time Parliament was involved in one of the periodic debates about the abolition of capital punishment, a point taken up by the advice column writers when they responded to my inquiry about a week later: 'We don't know why you should wish to apply for such a job – executioners will soon be going out of fashion. However, if you still wish to apply you should write to the Prison Commission, Horseferry House, Thorney Street, London SW1.'

I thought about it very seriously for several days; about the effect my becoming a hangman would have on Joyce, on my friends and on me. I thought about what I would have to do and the people I would be involved with. I also thought of my life at the pit and the unending sequence of mornings, afternoons and nights stretching away into the future. I wrote to the Prison Commission.

My letter was brief, not much longer than my note to the newspaper column had been:

Dear Sirs,
  I wish to apply for the position of assistant executioner. I am 26 years old and I am employed at the Sherwood Colliery in

Nottinghamshire as a welder. I am very interested in the study of crime and criminals, which is the thing that has led me to make this application. I feel sure that I could do the job. I hope you will consider my application favourably.'

I posted the letter in the village the same day as I wrote it – 23rd January 1947 – and prepared to wait. I thought such important matters would take time. I was in for a surprise, for it was only a week later when I heard the letterbox click and there on the mat lay a brown envelope, unmistakably official. The fact that it had come so quickly should have set warning bells ringing, but it did not and my hopes were sky-high as I carefully opened the envelope. In a second my ambition was shattered.

'Sir,
In reply to your letter of 23rd January, I am directed by the Prison Commissioners to inform you that a note has been made of your application but that it is not proposed at present to add to the list of persons already qualified to assist at executions. I am sir your obedient servant, J. Holt, Establishment Officer.'

What hurt as much as anything was that it was a pre-printed letter with gaps left for name and date, and those had been filled in by hand; they obviously has so many people applying to be hangmen that it was worth their while to have the rejection letters ready in advance! I put the letter away and forgot about it. I never wrote to the Commission again. Life continued in its unchanging routine at the pit, and that is where I was one autumn morning almost two years later. I was welding some ducting in the pit yard when I heard Joyce shouting to me. She was looking over the wooden fence, waving something in her hand. When I walked over she said, 'You've got to go to prison. You've got an interview next week.'

The letter had arrived a few minutes earlier; she had opened it and run straight down to the pit. This time it was not a pre-printed letter. Headed 'HM Prison Lincoln', it said; 'You are requested to attend this prison at 10.30 a.m. on Friday 8th October 1948 in order that you may be medically examined and interviewed with a view to ascertaining your fitness for the post of assistant executioner. If you are unable to attend at the time stated please inform me as soon as possible so that other arrangements may be made.' It was signed by the governor of the prison, Brigadier E.R. Paton-Walsh.

I felt elated as I tucked the envelope in my pocket and went back to my welding. Lincoln was about forty miles away and I knew I would be there next week to keep my appointment with Brigadier Paton-Walsh. The one thing that troubled me was what Joyce would say; she knew of course that I had applied but I do not suppose she imagined for a moment that anything would come of it. She had not made any comment at the pit yard fence and she had still not said anything on the Friday morning as I dressed in my best suit – a grey pin-stripe made years before by Grandad Thompson the tailor, but still a fine suit – and my most highly polished black shoes. In fact she did not need to tell me what she thought; she was hoping the whole thing would come to nothing.

So it was that a quarter of an hour after ten I stood before the high red-brick walls of Lincoln Prison. It was the first gaol I had ever seen and I thought it was tremendously impressive; the front had been built to look like a medieval castle and the gatehouse was flanked by octagonal towers which even had slit windows. There was a massive wooden gate with a small wicket in the left-hand side and I walked up to that and rapped on the iron knocker. A small hatch opened, a face appeared, then the hatch was slammed shut again. A moment later there was the sound of unlocking and the wicket opened. 'What do you want?' asked the warder who emerged.

I was nervous and handed him my letter without a word. He read it and then said, 'Come inside.'

As soon as I was through the gate, the wicket was locked behind me and I found myself standing between the main gate and another, iron, gate a few yards further into the prison. The warder led the way into the gatehouse office and left me, saying, 'Will you wait here a minute?'

In the office two warders were working at a desk, apparently going through record cards. They did not speak to me or acknowledge my presence. I sat on a wooden bench and looked around. The walls had once been yellow but were now almost brown with age and dirt. The warders, murmuring to each other, had black uniforms – not especially smart – with their keys hanging on long silver chains.

Several times during the ten minutes that I was left there, I found myself wondering what I had let myself in for, but I did not think of changing my mind and then it was too late anyway.

The first warder came back into the office and said, 'You can see the governor now. This way.'

Outside the office we walked up to the iron gate; a warder on the inside unlocked another small wicket and we stepped into the main part of the prison. As we walked away, I heard the wicket clang to and it was locked again.

I was surprised to find the inside of the prison as attractive as it was. As we walked the thirty yards towards the buildings which were obviously the hub of the gaol, we passed lawns and flowerbeds which were all well tended and quite colourful despite the time of year. I was becoming nervous as the interview with the governor approached, and things were not helped by the warder, who clearly was not interested in small talk with the likes of me and said not a single word. He led the way up a small flight of three or four steps and we came to a locked door. 'Open up!' he shouted, and there was rattling as the chap on the other side unlocked the door. We walked through and again there was banging and rattling as that was locked behind us. I was counting: three to break through if I wanted to get out in a hurry!

As we walked along the corridor there was a prisoner, an oldish man, on his hands and knees with a brush and a bucket of water, scrubbing the floor. The warder ploughed straight through and left me a few paces behind as I tried to avoid the area the man was cleaning. Without even looking at me he whispered quickly, 'Gizza fag! Gizza fag!' I just gawped at him. 'Gizza fag! Gizza fag!' he repeated urgently. It dawned on me at last what he was saying and I put my hand in my pocket, took a couple of Woodbines out of a packet, and casually dropped them. They landed in the water swimming around on the floor but quick as a flash the old lag scooped them up and whipped them out of sight.

I hurried to catch up with the warder, who was now standing at a doorway, looking at me. I do not know if he had seen my charitable donation to the old prisoner. If he had, he did not say anything.

I was shown into an office which was quite large but about as basic as it could possibly be. There was just a battered old wooden desk with a chair on my side and a chair on the other side. It was icy cold, so cold that it made me shiver. There was also in that room the smell, the prison smell. It is present and the same in every gaol from one end of the country to the other; an indescribable mixture of food, polish and sweaty bodies. It stayed in my nostrils for days.

The governor walked in a few moments later. Brigadier Paton-Walsh was a tall man, over six feet, with a distinctly military air despite the fact that he was wearing a suit. He looked stern and severe and there was no alteration in his expression as he went to the other side of the desk and sat down. He did not offer to shake hands but did tell me to sit, and the interview started.

The first few minutes went very badly. He was cold and intimidating with a commanding, confident air about him. I thought I had the air of the pit about me, and I felt my confidence oozing away.

'Why do you want to do this job?' he asked.

As he stared across the desk at me, I started to fumble the reply I had rehearsed over and over in the past week. 'I've always been interested in crime and criminals. I've spent a lot of time studying the subject and I have quite a collection of books.'

There was no reaction.

'I also feel sure I could do the job,' I added rather lamely.

I thought he might ask me about my collection of books but he ignored that remark and asked me several questions about my job.

'What about hobbies?' he asked.

'Well, as I said earlier, one of my main hobbies is reading about crime and I have quite a collection of books on the subject. Non-fiction books, not novels.'

This time he bit. 'What's in your collection?'

'There are some on forensic medicine. Others on famous crimes and criminals.'

But he was off in another direction. 'Are you interested in sport?'

'Not very much.'

'Not cricket or football?' he went on.

'No.'

I knew the interview was going very badly. There was no expression on his face but he was making me feel inferior. I thought I had blown it, so I thought bugger it, and said the most extraordinary thing. 'I do quite a bit of shooting.'

'Oh, where?'

'I belong to a rifle club in Mansfield. I also do quite a lot of pheasant shooting in Clumber Park and on the Welbeck Estate,' I replied, scarcely believing what I was telling the governor of one of His Majesty's prisons.

At first the remark did not click with him. 'Oh, do you shoot with the Duke?'

'No, I shoot when the Duke's gone to bed,' I replied.

For a moment I thought I had gone too far. I looked at that stern, austere man, and then suddenly an enormous smile spread over his face. He threw back his head and roared with laughter!

'Come in here, doc!' he bawled. 'We've got a poacher wants to be a hangman!'

The confession had quite broken the ice and the atmosphere changed completely. The doctor, who had obviously been earwigging outside during the interview, came in. He asked me a few funny questions which were obviously probing my psychological state, to make sure I was not a pervert trying to get his thrills with the government's help, and then he went on to give me a medical.

'Are you deft?' the governor asked.

His accent was so upper-class that for split second I misunderstood and thought he had asked me, 'Are you daft?'

I thought I must be, to get myself into this, but replied, 'Yes, I'm pretty good with my hands. I have to be for my job.'

There were a few more questions and then Brigadier Paton-Walsh said something that I was always to remember: 'If you are appointed to this job, you will be a servant of the law carrying out the sentence of the law. No sentiment must ever enter your conduct during an execution.' He went on to say that if my application was successful I would be hearing from the Prison Commissioners in due course. With that he pressed a bell on the desk to call a warder and the interview was over. As I said goodbye he did not look so severe. He may even have had a twinkle in his eye!

In a few moments I was outside the main prison gate, free again in the outside world. I drew some deep breaths of air and headed home, where I found Joyce bursting to know what had happened.

I told her, 'Well it looks as if I'm going to be an assistant executioner.'

I'll never forget her reaction. 'Good God! What will me Mam say!'

It was to be some time before we found out the answer to that particular question, although six weeks later, I learned that I had got through the interview. When another of the brown envelopes arrived, this one was headed Pentonville Prison.

'You have been selected to attend the course of instruction for assistant executioners. I should be glad if you would kindly let me know if it is your intention to attend the course.'

I kindly let him know that it was my intention to attend the course.

3 The Mysteries

A few minutes past two o'clock on the afternoon of Monday 6th December 1948, just three weeks before my twenty-eighth birthday, I found myself standing at attention in the governor's office at Pentonville Prison. Three other aspiring hangmen were ranged alongside me: George Dickinson, a young mathematician with a big chemical firm in Manchester, William Pollard, a thirty-six-year-old Londoner who worked at the Woolwich Arsenal, and Harry Allen, an ice-cream salesman from Birmingham. Harry was the oldest, in his late thirties, and he was to become a great friend.

The governor sat behind a big desk, surrounded by warders and prison personnel. One glance was enough to reveal that he clearly operated in less austere surroundings than his provincial opposite number in Lincolnshire; the office was much larger and noticeably cleaner and warmer. He spoke to us briefly about the training week, mentioning that there would be written and practical tests on Friday, and then he introduced Mr Hughes, a quite elderly prison warder, who was to be our instructor.

At the end of his talk, he said, 'There is one other matter which I must bring to your attention. It is customary in these matters ...'

He paused and smiled.

'It is customary in these matters to observe the element of secrecy at all times. You will in due course be subject to the Official Secrets Act. It would be better for practical purposes if you regarded yourselves as governed by the Act even now.'

He looked sternly at us for a moment. 'I need not emphasize that the authorities would take a very dim view of the matter if any of you were to speak or write of the things that you see or learn during your week with us.'

We were suitably impressed by the threat and someone muttered, 'Yes, sir.'

'Good,' he smiled. 'Any questions?'

'Yes sir,' I piped up. 'Harry Allen and me haven't got any accommodation. We wondered if we could stay in the prison?'

The governor half-turned to one of the senior warders and chuckled. 'We do have a large amount of accommodation here but I'm afraid it's all fully occupied!'

Everyone laughed at the governor's joke, then one of the warders said, 'They could try the Union Jack Club, sir.'

'Yes, give them the details later,' replied the governor, in a way that indicated the interview was over.

With Mr Hughes leading the way, we travelled through the prison until we arrived outside a door on the first landing level in one of the wings. A warder unlocked it and we followed Hughes inside; the door banged shut behind us and the key rattled in the lock. We found ourselves in a large, roomy cell, unremarkable at a first glance apart from its size. There was a single bed under the window, a table and a few chairs. As I looked around, the only thing which did seem strange was the window; it was barred of course, but there was also wire-netting on the inside.

'Take a seat lads,' said Hughes.

With a shortage of chairs, Harry and I sat on the edge of the bed as Hughes explained, 'This'll be your classroom for the week … it's the condemned cell.'

I think we were all shattered! It was not at all what we had imagined. It was so ordinary.

After a moment's silence, as we looked anew at our surroundings, Harry said, 'I didn't think it would be like this.'

'What were you expecting – a dungeon?' laughed Hughes.

He nodded towards a closed door on my left. 'Through there is a bathroom and then beyond that is a second condemned cell. We can't go through because it's locked, but it's identical to this one.'

To my right was a pair of doors painted yellow. Hughes walked across and pushed them open; we followed. There was a narrow corridor, only a couple of paces wide, and then another pair of yellow doors which he pushed open. 'This is where we drop 'em.'

Ten paces had taken us from the condemned man's bed into the execution chamber! I was astounded.

The gallows room was identical in size to the condemned cell; that is to say, like two normal cells joined into one. All that was to be seen was the great beam over the centre of the room, which did not have a rope hanging from it then; the operating lever, which looked like something out of a railway signalling box; and the massive trapdoors which seemed to take up most of the floor. They were impressive, far bigger than anything I had expected.

As we stood looking around, it was clear that the one thing the execution chamber did not lack was atmosphere. It had a noticeable effect on all of us.

I looked back through the doors to the condemned cell … it was just amazing. I had read practically everything published about hanging and I fancied myself well informed; none of it had prepared me for this. 'I thought there was an execution shed,' I remarked to Hughes.

'It's years since there were execution sheds,' he replied, 'although most of the papers still haven't realized yet! This is the standard set-up in all the prisons now. It gets the business over in a fraction of the time.'

At that, he turned and started walking towards a corner of the execution chamber to indicate that the question session was ended for the time being and we should continue the tour of the suite. Near the wall he lifted a small trapdoor to reveal a narrow flight of steps leading down into the drop. He went ahead of us and turned a light on so that as we went down we could see that we were not descending into a pit but into another room of the same size as the execution chamber.

The trap doors were now high above our heads, although there was nothing to be seen of the operating mechanism. On the walls of this room were four steel springs. Hughes explained. 'These hold the trap doors when they drop down. They catch the doors and stop them banging down against the walls and then bouncing back and hitting the man – after all, we don't want to knock him about, do we?'

It had about it the air of a joke which had been told many times before, but it created a vivid picture and was greeted with very, very weak smiles.

In the drop room there were two doorways. One was in the outside wall of the prison and I learned later that this was used to take the bodies out into the grounds for burial. Hughes took us through the other doorway and we found ourselves in a strange room, the centrepiece of which was an enormous slab table which was covered with lead and had a gutter all the way round it. There were also a couple of sinks with taps on the wall and a cupboard. That was about it.

'This is the post-mortem room,' said Hughes. 'After the execution, the pathologists have to have a look at him.'

I found the room a thoroughly chilling place, and I have to say that with no access to a toilet – the condemned cell lavatory remained locked all week – the post-mortem room sinks saw service of a kind which would no doubt have shocked the pathologists!

Back in the condemned cell, Hughes gave us our first lecture.

'Hanging is efficient, clean and above all very, very quick. As you can see, the distance the man has to be moved between his cell and the gallows is short and once the trap doors are opened and he goes down, he's killed instantly by having his neck broken.'

He smiled. 'For any of you who is anatomically minded, it parts the second and third vertebrae. The fact that it is so fast is a kindness to the man who has to go and to the people who have to be present at an execution. It also means that so far as the hangmen are concerned, they have to know exactly what they're doing and they have to get it right first time. There is no margin for error – remember that.'

I knew I would.

Satisfied that we had noted his words, he continued, 'The gallows is tested the afternoon before the hanging by the executioners. On the day itself, they enter the cell at the appointed hour, strap the man's arms behind his back and take him through. The number one leads and the assistant follows behind the man. If there's likely to be trouble there'll be people around to help.'

No-one said a word.

'As assistant your job will be to strap his ankles and get yourself off the trap; the number one will do everything else. If you're still mucking about when he's ready, the number one will tap you on the shoulder and then you don't bugger about … you get off or go down – and it's a nasty drop even if you haven't got a rope round your neck!'

He smiled mirthlessly. 'If you've got it right, you'll still be standing in the execution chamber and the bloke won't … he'll be hanging on the end of the rope with his neck broken.'

The smile faded. 'It's got to be right, there can't be any mistakes. Christ knows what would happen to the condemned man and Christ knows what would happen to the bloke who was responsible for it! It's got to be right first time – get that.'

He looked around the room to make sure we had all got it. The silence and the sombre expressions must have convinced him because he relaxed and we called it a day.

Darkness had fallen by the time we stood again in the fresh, cool, air of the winter's afternoon. We parted outside the prison gates, Pollard went home, Dickinson was apparently staying with relatives, and Harry and I headed off in search of accommodation.

The Union Jack Club turned out to be a servicemen's hostel with no frills and few comforts. It supplied a roof and a clean bed in a room which was smaller than the cells in the prison, but at a reasonable price; they told us it would be fifteen shillings for the week, without meals. It was not the sort of place to spend a cosy evening, so Harry and I put our cases in our rooms and strolled through the streets in search of a more congenial atmosphere. We were soon ensconced in a quiet corner in a pub near Hyde Park.

'I was hoping to meet Albert Pierrepoint,' said Harry.

'Me, too,' I agreed. 'But I suppose it was a bit unlikely that he would be able to spend the whole week with the likes of us. He could even be otherwise engaged this week!'

'I suppose we will eventually meet him – if we pass the exam!' laughed Harry.

'If we pass the exam,' I agreed. 'Still, I'm just pleased to be here.'

'How many times did you apply?' he asked.

'Once. Why, how many times did you apply?'

'Eighteen,' he replied cheerfully.

'Eighteen times!' I exclaimed. 'You applied eighteen times? Don't you ever give up?'

'I think I gave up after I'd been turned down a couple of times, but writing the letters just became a habit. I always hoped I would apply at the right time.'

I looked at Harry with a new respect.

When we arrived in the execution suite on the second day, we found a couple of additions: two black wooden boxes with broad white arrows painted on the lids. One of the boxes was about two feet by three feet; the second was smaller. Both had heavy padlocks. Hughes opened the smaller of the boxes first. It contained just a couple of lengths of steel chain and a set of pulley blocks.

The other box was more interesting. Inside were ropes, linen hoods and a number of straps. There were also some bits and pieces which had no significance for me then: copper wire, thread and chalk.

As we looked on, Hughes removed the equipment and laid it on the floor. It quickly became apparent that there were two of everything. He told us that the gear was normally kept in a store at Wandsworth Prison in London and then, as soon as a gaol anywhere in the country received a prisoner under sentence of death, the boxes were despatched by normal passenger train, with the keys posted by registered mail to the governor of the prison.

The ropes puzzled me. One was clean – in fact it was white – but the other was quite brown and dirty. I asked Hughes about that. He picked up the dirty rope and handed it to me. 'Oh, this one's been used,' he said casually. 'The government can't afford a new rope for every hanging!'

I looked at the rope and wondered how many men had been hanged with this. Hughes smiled at the look on my face. 'Some ropes are used time and time again – less stretch in them than new ropes. The rope's made of best Italian hemp,' he said, taking it from me. 'At each end there's a brass eye. One end is attached to a chain which hangs down from the beam. The noose is formed by the rope running through the other eye … no hangman's knot.'

Holding the noose up for us to have a look at, he continued, 'You'll notice that the last couple of feet of the rope – the bit that forms the noose – has leather sewn around the rope. That's to minimize the damage to the man's neck,' he said, smirking at his own sense of humour. 'Without this leather there'd be nasty rope burns but as it is there's very little marking.'

Equipping the gallows with a noose was the work of but a few moments. Taking a length of chain from the small black box, Hughes went up a stepladder to the beams. On top of the beams was a pair of brackets which had a pin slotted through. Hughes partially withdrew the pin and then slotted it back into position through one of the links of the chain so that when he'd finished the chain hung down between the beams. Descending a few steps, he shackled the rope to the end of the chain. Several feet of the rope were now lying on the floor but he carefully collected the slack in a series of loops at a height of about six feet and got Dickinson to fasten them in place with a length of thread from the box. The noose was hanging at head height.

'You aim to get the noose hanging at just the right height to slip over the man's head,' said Hughes. 'Every split second counts.'

Taking hold of the noose he continued, 'When the man goes down, the packthread snaps.' He gave the noose a sharp tug, the thread parted with an audible ping and the gathered loops of the rope fell down to the floor.

'Why not attach the rope straight to the beam?' I asked, as Hughes gathered the rope up again.

'The distance your man is going to have to drop to break his neck depends mainly on his weight,' replied Hughes. 'If he's fifteen stone he obviously doesn't have to fall as far as, say, a ten-stone chap. You therefore need to be able to adjust the equipment to meet his requirements. The chain is hanging below the beam, you can lengthen or shorten the drop.'

With the rope tied back up again, he selected William Pollard to demonstrate the art of noosing. 'Hands in your pockets, William,' he said, pushing him into position in the middle of the trap. In a flash he whipped a hood out of his pocket, pulled it over the unfortunate Pollard's head, flicked the noose over and it was tight round his neck.

We all roared with laughter as a torrent of muffled swearing came from the hooded head of Pollard.

'You're all right William – calm down,' Hughes reassured him. 'The rest of you can stop laughing because you're all going to go through it as well.'

'It's important to get the brass eye under the left jaw,' he continued, indicating its postition on William. 'The rope's got to be tight – but on the other hand you're not trying to strangle the man. There's a rubber ring on the rope and once you've got the noose in the correct position, bring the ring down so that it holds it in position.'

'Ok William, you can come out now,' he said, tapping Pollard on the arm. The Londoner clawed the rope loose from around his throat and pulled the bag off his head. There was another burst of laughter as his face appeared. 'Bloody hell! You could have warned me.' He took a deep breath. 'It wasn't the rope but the bag that half scared me to death – what the hell is that for?'

'Traditionally, it's to give the condemned man some dignity in death. These days I suppose it's useful because it stops them seeing what's happening in the last split second,' explained Hughes. 'If they could see the number one going for the lever they might faint or try and jump off the trap – which could shift the position of the noose.'

The rest of the morning we spent learning the techniques of strapping arms and legs. Hughes stressed that while the straps should be fastened to prevent the man getting free, the restraint was to be quite light and should not hurt or panic the man. Arms were strapped at the wrists, legs just above the ankles.

For the next two hours and indeed on and off for the next 3½ days, we practised. We practised on each other; we practised on chair legs; at any spare moment we practised. And always there was Hughes there: 'You've got to be quick. You've got to be quick. Speed it up. Do it faster. Not bad – do it again.'

Indeed, it sounds a simple matter to get those straps on, but even with the most co-operative condemned men there could ever have been – that is to say, each other – that first morning we were pretty bad.

We lunched in the warders' mess, and were served by convicts. No-one spoke to us and it was a dismal affair with quite gruesome food. I was pleased to get back to the condemned cell, and the afternoon was to provide some strange experiences.

It started off as a continuation of the strapping practice of the morning, but then Hughes said we would be doing a run-through of part of the procedure. In the execution chamber he gave Harry a tape-measure and told him to find the middle of the trap. I held the end as Harry measured. The trap was 7 feet 6 inches wide and Harry indicated the 3 feet 9 inches mark. Hughes bent down and chalked a figure T on the wooden trap doors. He pointed up. 'The rope hangs exactly in the centre of the drop. You've got to get the prisoner exactly in the centre too. You don't guess it – you measure it. He's only got to be an inch or two off-centre and he'll swing like a bloody pendulum when he's dropped. Put him on that chalk mark and he's in the right place.'

In the condemned cell he gave us our orders. 'George – you're the condemned man. Syd's the number one, William's the assistant and Harry can be the parson.'

We assumed our positions. William and I backed up to the cell door, George sat down at the table with his back to us, while Harry, the parson, sat opposite him. 'Right!' said Hughes and we went into action. Harry, with an ear-to-ear grin, was in the process of 'blessing' the condemned man when we reached him and tapped him on the shoulder. George rose to his feet and we quickly strapped his arms behind him. I led the way into the execution chamber and (pure luck) stopped him bang on the chalk mark. With some fumbling I got the bag over his head and the rope slipped on easily. William meanwhile was having trouble getting the leg strap on.

'Tap him on the shoulder!' roared Hughes at me. I leant across and tapped. 'Get off the drop!' screamed Hughes.

Pollard threw himself back at the same instant as I leapt over and touched the black lever. With the action and noise it was almost a surprise that nothing happened.

'Bloody close-run thing was that!' said Hughes to Pollard. 'I reckon there was damn near two of you went down the hole that time. You've got to be quick!'

Then it was my turn to be the victim of George and Harry. William sat it out – after Harry's efforts it was decided to abandon parsons.

The same procedure but this time it's different, this time I'm being hanged and the first time it's terrifying. There's the tap on your shoulder ... you start to rise and they have your arms behind your back ... the straps are on and you can't do a thing, you're helpless ... they turn you and there's the noose hanging through in the other room and you're walking towards it ... closer ... you're in the execution chamber, and the hangman stops you and you're standing on the trapdoor ... then it's so dark ... hood on the face ... things going on you can't see ... something tightening round the legs ... noose round the neck ... something under the chin ... hard to breathe ...scuffling ...

'Don't press that sodding lever!' It seemed a long time before the noose slackened and they took the bag off.

The experience was a truly frightening one but after all, we were in the execution chamber at Pentonville Prison, and innumerable people had been hanged in this room and we were doing it almost for real. Were there not just two safety devices preventing that lever being moved over and the trapdoors opening?

Practice, practice and more practice. 'This time Harry's the number one, Syd's the assistant and William's for the drop.'

And always the same urgency: 'Speed it up! We can do it faster. Try again. Don't worry about his hairstyle – get the bloody hood on! When you get that tap you get off the trap! You've got to be quick. Carry on at this speed and your customers are going to die of old age – ripe old age!'

Eventually, though, it did start to come together and as the afternoon wore on and the daylight outside the condemned cell window faded, we began to get faster. The seeds of competition had been planted too; it was becoming important to be quicker than the others and seconds clipped from previous best times were a cause of satisfaction for the number one and his assistant.

That evening Harry and I discussed our progress when we had found ourselves a quiet corner of yet another pub. We had asked the other two, as we left the jail, if they would like to join us for a drink, but they said they weren't able to and so it was just the pair of us again. Harry felt the other two were being a bit uppish. Dickinson, I thought, was snooty, but perhaps we were being unkind to William because for him it had been a bad day, which must have shaken his confidence considerably.

'God, it even had me jumping when Hughes screamed at him to get off the trap that first time – and I was only the parson,' grinned Harry.

Day Three.

The dummy runs and strapping practice started immediately, but on one of the dry runs – I was the condemned man – Hughes suddenly shouted, 'You don't want to go!'

The order came just as the executioners arrived behind me. I started to go away from them but they were too close and they were able to grab my arms and yank them up behind my back. Struggle as hard as I might, I couldn't get free and once they'd got the strap on my wrists I was helpless and they were able to frogmarch me off to the gallows.

The fireworks came a couple of hangings later. Harry was the condemned man, George the executioner and William the assistant. This time the hangmen had only just started to walk towards the back of the condemned man when the order to resist came. I gaped in astonishment as Harry threw himself clear over the table, swung round and stood on the other side with a maniacal grin on his face. The advancing hangmen faltered and shuffled to a stop in amazement.

'Don't just stand there, get the bugger!' bellowed Hughes.

Galvanized into action, Dickinson made a grab across the table, but one pace back and Harry was out of trouble. The hangmen re-group and start a pincer movement around the ends of the table. Harry, still with a mile-wide grin, is creeping back as fast as they're creeping forward. The hangmen make a dash but Harry flicks a chair into the path of the advancing Dickinson who manages to parry the flying furniture but hurtles off to the left trying to regain his balance and stay on his feet. Harry, meanwhile, has made his big mistake: backed over the end of the bed and gone down in a heap on the mattress. William is on him in an instant – but he hasn't got the strap. Dickinson arrives to join the fray and there's a hell of a bundle on the bed with legs, arms, heads and bodies turning up everywhere.

I was helpless with laughter when Hughes suddenly turned on me and said, 'You're a big prison warder – go and help them!'

Trying to control my laughter, I got over to the scene of the battle but it was quite obvious that the hanging wasn't going to take place – at least not in the foreseeable future. By this time Harry was under George and William, lying on his side with, as far as I could make out, his hands jammed tight between his legs, or somebody's hands jammed between his legs, the whole heap of bodies still bouncing around all over the bed. I grabbed the strap, which had fallen to the floor, and was standing poised to get it round one of Harry's wrists in the event of it somehow coming to the surface, when Hughes brought the pantomime to a close.

As the heavily panting and sweating execution party took a ten-minute breather and lit up, several things were apparent. First, from the murderous looks which were being aimed at Harry from Dickinson and Pollard, relations which hadn't been exactly warm to this point were taking a distinct turn for the worse. Second, from the size of Harry's grin, he thought he'd shown them a thing or two and it served them damn well right for being snooty with him. Third, and most important when it came to a real hanging, get the armstrap on and the condemned man's opportunity to resist was cut to negligible proportions, as I had found out, but if he cut up rough before that strap was on there were all the makings of a fiasco.

I thought Harry might have gone too far, but Hughes had obviously enjoyed the entertainment and the wily old devil may well have read the situation which existed and had a pretty good idea of what would happen when he gave Harry that order to fight.

After dinner we saw the gallows in operation for the first time. The 'victim' was a dummy – a three-foot-high canvas bag with a leather ball sewed on for a head. It was filled with sand and weighed about sixty or seventy pounds. Hughes explained that it was normally used to test the gallows.

He positioned it on the chalk mark in the centre of the drop, wrapped a towel round its skinny neck so that it was nearer the size of a human neck, and put the noose on. Telling us to get off the trap, he walked over to the lever and removed the cotter through the end of the safety pin and then the pin itself.

With a final look to check that everyone was clear, he said, 'Now you'll see what happens.'

He pushed the lever over. The whole floor seemed to collapse as those great trapdoors went down with a boom which must have been heard all over the wing of the prison. There was a blur as the sandbag, like some condemned dwarf, plunged six feet and stopped dead.

There was an unnatural silence as my ears recovered from the boom. In the pit which had appeared, the sandbag was hanging below us, the leather head pushed slightly over to one side. Both rope and bag were quite still – no bounce or swing. It required no imagination at all to realize what would have happened if it had been a man on the end of the rope instead of a canvas bag.

Hughes nodded at the canvas dwarf. 'If we'd been doing it for real, our friend there would be left where he is for an hour and we'd be off for our breakfast. As it is, we'll give him a reprieve.'

With the help of a set of pulleys, which were hooked on to the chain hanging down from the beam, we spent the next few minutes recovering the canvas bag and hauling the trapdoors back into position. As soon as they were back up and the lever re-set, Hughes very carefully put the safety pin back in and the cotter through the end.

Thursday, the final day of our training.

In the morning Hughes dispensed the last of his knowledge; he taught us how to calculate the drop we would have to give to kill a condemned man and kill him cleanly and quickly. He explained that there was a table of drops, but that was only issued to executioners and even he did not have one. We would have to work it out for ourselves. The rough formula is the weight of the man in pounds, divided into a thousand, equals the drop in feet and inches. Thus a 10 stone man – 140 pounds – gets a drop of 7 feet 1¾ inches.

Rigging the equipment once you'd worked out the drop was surprisingly easy. First you had to measure 13 inches on the rope from the centre of the brass eye and mark it with chalk – that was standard allowance for the noose. The distance the man was to fall was measured from that chalk mark, so another 7 feet 1¾ inches along the rope and another chalk mark. If the man was 5 feet 6 inches tall, the chains had to be adjusted so that the second chalk mark was at that height. The rope's neatly tied up and the noose will slip gently over his head.

We spent a couple of hours working out the drops of mythical condemned men of various weights. Maths was one of my best subjects at school, so it posed no problems for me, and for Dickinson, a mathematician, it was child's play. It didn't appear to be quite so easy for Pollard and Harry. Hughes made the lesson more interesting by occasionally telling a couple of us to rig a particular drop.

In the afternoon, with the time now slipping away, we practised the lot. We worked out drops, rigged the gallows, strapped arms and led each other to the trapdoors. There was now an assuredness about what we were doing and as that confidence grew we began to leave our teacher behind. Hughes was no longer leading; he had become an observer. As the afternoon drew to a close, I had no doubts that we had the skills to hang a man; whether we ever would remained to be decided after our performance before the governor.

That night Harry and I lived it up. It was our last night together and who could tell when we might meet again – if ever.

We ate out, fish and chips with all the trimmings, and after those dreadful prison meals it was wonderful; I can seldom remember enjoying a meal quite as much as that one.

Friday, decision day.

We took the written examination first thing in the morning. Hughes handed each of us a paper and told us we had thirty minutes to complete it.

Question 1: What drop would you allow a man who weighed 12½ stones?

Twelve and half stones is 175 pounds divided into 1,000 equals 5 feet 8½ inches.

Question 2: Explain in your own words the duties of an executioner and an assistant executioner.

How to start? I looked at that blank sheet of paper on which so much depended and then I had a stroke of pure inspiration – the governor at Lincoln Prison!

'The most important thing to be remembered is that the executioner and his assistant are servants of the law carrying out the sentence of the law,' I wrote. 'No sentiment must ever enter their conduct.'

After that it was easy. I ran through the procedure and outlined the parts played by the number one and the assistant, and rounded off my answer with a couple of sentences about them having to be sober and discreet and not draw attention to themselves.

Feeling as smug as hell, I sat back ten minutes before the end of the exam. Dickinson and Pollard were still writing away. Harry looked worried. Hughes had wandered off into the execution chamber and Harry pointed at his exam paper: What drop would you allow a man who weighed 11 stone 2 pounds?

Harry was having trouble with his sums! I picked up my pen, worked it out and scribbled 6 feet 5 for him. I knew I had a friend for life as Harry's frown disappeared. A few minutes later Hughes collected the papers.

The practical test before the governor wasn't until half past two in the afternoon, so we spent the rest of the morning practising. I strapped chair legs, hanged people, helped to hang people and was a customer myself. Most of the time we were by ourselves; Hughes had disappeared with the examination papers and was away for almost an hour.

Just before lunch he told us about the test. 'There'll be just one run through in front of the governor – so get it right. Syd you'll be the number one, Harry you'll be the assistant, and George you're the condemned man. William will be sitting it out.'

Pollard's face dropped. Over lunch we tried to console him and tell him that it didn't mean anything at all. The truth was, we all knew what it meant – and that included him.

When Harry and I found ourselves alone for a moment he muttered, 'Thanks.'

'Don't mention it,' I said. 'You want to worry about this afternoon. We could be in the soup if we muck it up.'

'We'll be OK,' he replied.

'I hope Dickinson doesn't cause us any problems,' I said, less sure than him. 'We could look a couple of nits if he decides to give the governor a show and play the reluctant hero.'

'He won't,' said Harry with one of his big grins. 'I've already had a word with him and I've told him we'll kill him if anything goes wrong!'

I laughed. 'If anything goes wrong we probably will!'

In the event, the hanging was a sensation. The governor and the engineer officer turned up to watch the demonstration. We got into our positions: George was sitting at the table; Harry and I were standing at the door. The engineer officer was holding a stopwatch.

'Right,' said the governor, 'away you go.' We strode quickly over to George who looked over his shoulder and rose to his feet as we got to him. With no more than a light touch from us, he had his hands up behind his back and we had the strap on.

I turned and led the way into the execution chamber, striding across the trapdoors with George following me and Harry a pace behind him. George stood bang on the chalk mark in the centre of the drop so I didn't have to worry about that and I quickly got the hood over his head. Harry was on his knees fixing the legstrap as I slipped the noose over George's head and pulled the ring down roughly to get it done.

I didn't have to warn Harry to get clear. He'd finished and was moving off the trap with a wink! I threw myself at the lever and was just about to tap it when the governor shouted: 'Stop!'

I looked at him in amazement. His face was white. By God, he thought it was real – he thought we were going to do it!

The engineer officer was looking at his stopwatch. 'Forty-five seconds, sir.'

I felt a sense of elation. It was about the fastest run we'd done and it was good enough to convince the governor that he was watching the real thing. He still looked ruffled. As we took the noose and hood off George, it kept going through my mind: 'He really thought we were going to hang the bastard!'

That was the end of our training. I felt quite sad as we packed the equipment away and tidied up the condemned cell and execution chamber. We seemed to have been together for a long time. We said goodbye to Hughes and thanked him for his help during the week. We left him in the condemned cell and another warder took us to the main gate.

I was never to see William Pollard again. He disappeared into the gloom on that winter's afternoon and nothing more was ever heard of him again in hanging circles.

Dickinson's career as a hangman was brief and disastrous. He passed the test, because he went on a job at Swansea Prison and I had the story later from Pierrepoint. The execution went well enough ... the problems occurred when Pierrepoint gave him a lift home to Manchester.

Pierrepoint told me, 'We were driving back to Manchester. He looked a bit white and he was saying hardly anything. Then all of a sudden he groaned and the bugger was sitting their pissing himself!'

Pierrepoint stopped the car and got him out in the air. After a few minutes he said he was well enough to continue and off they went. They hadn't done twenty miles before it happened again, and it happened a third time before they got home.

Both Dickinson and the car were in a state by the time they got to Manchester and a relieved Pierrepoint was able to get rid of him – determined that Dickinson would never take part in another execution.

He didn't have to bother. Dickinson quit his job, uprooted his family and emigrated – we heard to Canada.

Harry made it, and he figures again in our story. I passed the test and I lasted longer than any of them. I hit trouble in the end – but a lot was to happen before then.

4   The Real Thing

Things began to move quickly in the new year; on 18th January I had a letter from the Prison Commissioners which told me that I had been successful. There was also an agreement to be signed and witnessed. It was wrapped up in legal language but the drift of the document was simple enough; it was all about secrecy. I was forbidden to give any information about an execution to any unauthorized person or persons. I was barred from writing a book, newspaper or magazine article. I was not to take part in lectures, displays, exhibitions, or cinema films!

I signed the document in front of the local police inspector and was bound to the King for the sum of £50.

A month later, I was officially notified that I was a hangman. At least, my name had been added to the list of people competent to act as an assistant executioner. The letter informed me that assistant executioners were employed as required by the governor of the prison where the execution was to take place and when my services were required a communication would be sent to me. I was warned: 'There is no necessity for you to write to any sheriff or under-sheriff asking for employment with an execution and any such application may result in your name being struck off the list.'

The letter concluded with yet another order to keep my mouth shut. 'The Prison Commission desire to emphasize the importance of complete reticence in regard to your official duties.'

The Prison Commissioners obviously did not rate the comprehension of their executioners that highly! They were tight too, as I was to discover the following month when I was invited to witness the execution of James Farrell. The invitation made it clear that as I would not be required to take an active part in the proceedings, no fees would be payable. Their attitude

48

irritated me. I might not be taking part but I still had to be there on the afternoon before the hanging and I was going to lose two days' pay! I made up my mind to take it further.

The events at Winson Green came as a revelation. Pierrepoint and Kirk were just amazing. When they rigged the gallows before the execution they worked silently and seemed to understand each other without need of words.

Since receiving the invitation to witness the execution, I had been looking forward to the night at the prison with a mixture of anticipation and unease. I was looking forward to spending an evening in the company of the famous hangman, Albert Pierrepoint, but I could only guess what a prison would be like on the eve of an execution; it was surely going to be a dreadfully dismal and tense place.

Shocking as it may sound, the truth is that we spent as jolly an evening as it was possible to have. Away from the execution chamber, Pierrepoint and Kirk relaxed and seemed completely unworried by either the job in the morning or their surroundings. Both of them were pub landlords; Pierrepoint had the curiously-named "Help the Poor Struggler" at Hollinwood near Manchester and Kirk had "The Black Horse" at Elton near Peterborough. Both had the easy way of publicans. Harry Kirk was an extrovert who had done any number of things in this time, including being a policeman and an attendant in a lunatic asylum, and he could talk on any subject under the sun. He took a shine to me straight away, referring to me as 'Young 'un', and he called me that ever afterwards.

Pierrepoint was slightly more reserved to begin with, but good company. I had once seen him described in the *News of the World* as 'The jovial hangman'; he certainly was that evening. His blue eyes twinkled as he swapped tales and stories with Kirk in his marked Lancashire accent. I was overawed by the situation, and the two men, and was content just to be there and to listen to them.

Kirk, with his seemingly endless stream of jokes, rude and otherwise, was the life and soul of the gathering, yet Pierrepoint was the number one and effortlessly conveyed his authority. When Pierrepoint spoke, everyone listened.

Strangely, there were two things they never referred to at all. One was the job they would be doing in the morning; the other was the man just a couple of hundred yards away in the prison who now had less than twelve hours to live.

Eventually, during a lull in the converation towards the end of the evening, I touched on the subject obliquely. 'It's very quiet in the prison, isn't it?'

'It's 'cos they bloody well know what's going to happen in the morning,' said Pierrepoint forcefully. He gave me a look and I dropped the subject.

Shortly afterwards, with our allowance of two pint bottles of beer drunk and the conversation dying out, Pierrepoint said he was turning in, and that was the signal for all of us to get to bed. It was ten o'clock – the man in the condemned cell now had just eleven hours to live.

James Farrell duly paid for his crimes the next morning and the speed at which that frightened young man was put to death was quite unimaginable. Needless to say, the Albert Pierrepoint with the twinkling eyes and the Harry Kirk with the inexhaustible fund of funny stories had vanished. That morning we were in the company of two completely different men – serious, cold and ruthlessly efficient. During the night, while we slept, the pub landlords had been replaced by the state hangmen.

A couple of days later the memories had taken on a dreamlike quality. I found it difficult to believe that I had really been there and really seen the execution. The sense of unreality was heightened by the knowledge that the next time I was contacted by the authorities, it would not be as a trainee; the next letter would be to call on the services of an assistant executioner.

Come payday, though, there were more down-to-earth matters to be considered; to whit, my lighter wage packet as a result of the two-day unpaid trip to Birmingham. I had raised the fact that I wasn't being paid with Albert Pierrepoint, but he'd been unsympathetic. 'That's normal,' he told me. 'That's the way it was for me too.'

Caution urged that I should let the matter drop ... but a Nottinghamshire pitman and his money are not so easily parted! I simmered for a few days and then wrote to the Prison Commissioners. I knew I was taking a chance but I thought bugger it, I'll try for expenses. To this day I do not know if my letter touched the better side of their nature or just caught them on the hop, but a few days later I was informed that they had reconsidered. I was to get an assistant executioner's fee of three guineas!

That was the good news. The bad news showed another side to

the Prison Commissioners and the way that they treated their hangmen. I realized that I was soon going to have to face the problem of getting time off from the pit. So far I had managed to take the days off for the interview, training week and execution of James Farrell, as holiday and at short notice, but the pit manager, Jock Reid, was not going to wear that sort of behaviour for long. It seemed to me that the most impressive way for the problem to be solved was for the Prison Commissioners to contact me and explain the situation. In my letter about expenses, I put the suggestion forward.

Their response to that was brief and frosty: 'The Commissioners are not prepared to approach your employers about your absence from work to attend executions and wish to point out that it is your responsibility to make the necessary arrangements to attend executions as and when required to do so. In this connection you are reminded that the rules require assistant executioners to maintain reticence in regard to their official duties.'

Priceless! They were telling me that I had to get my bosses to agree to me slipping away every now and again for a couple of days, at short notice, but I could not tell them what it was about. I knew that was not going to be well received by Jock Reid, and I decided to put off going to see him for as long as I could.

Officialdom clearly had mixed feelings about its hangmen, but I was soon to find out that as far as ordinary people were concerned, they were real celebrities. The name of Pierrepont was one of the most well known in the land, and after the executions of Nazi war criminals, in Europe too. Albert's pub was the most famous tavern in England and Harry Kirk had told me that the sightseers flocked to the place in thousands to gawp at the hangman.

I was curious to see Albert's pub, The Struggler, and, if the truth is told, I thought it would do me no harm at all to be in the good books of the number one. The railway company ran regular Saturday excursion trips from the Mansfield area to the funfair and zoo at Manchester's Belle Vue Park, and so a couple of months after the Farrell job I joined a five-bob special. My only interest was in getting to Pierrepoint's pub, but when I phoned him a couple of days before the trip I told him I was going to Belle Vue and just might manage to get along and have a quick drink. He seemed friendly and pleased to hear from me, and said, 'Do get along if you can.'

The excursion arrived at Belle Vue in the middle of the afternoon, so I did have a couple of hours in the park before I caught a bus into Manchester and went on to Pierrepoint's pub.

The Struggler was five miles out of the centre of the city on the road to Oldham, number 303, Manchester Road, Hollinwood. It must have been a village at some time and I suppose there was even a wood but if any of it had survived I did not see a trace of it; Hollinwood itself had long since been gobbled up by the expanding city. As the trolley-bus rolled along, there was no break in the red-brick Victorian buildings; for the most part, endless terraces of small, dark houses with front doors opening directly onto the footpath. The cobbled side streets were lined with the same small houses, jammed in as tight as could be. When the conductor told me we had arrived, Hollinwood turned out to be a stretch of the road like all the rest. The trolley-bus rolled on its way and I stood looking across the road at The Struggler, the most famous pub in England. It was the biggest building on the block, but built of just the same red brick as all the little houses and shops around it. The name was carved in a stone at roof level. It was not very impressive.

As I walked across the road, the hubbub of voices coming through the door indicated that although it was only seven o'clock, there was already a large crowd of people inside. I headed for the taproom and, as luck would have it, that was where I found Pierrepoint behind the bar chatting to some of his cronies. It was an odd sensation to see him in that setting after our last meeting.

No-one took any notice of me as I walked to the bar, until Albert looked up. 'Hello Syd – you made it,' he said with a smile and that friendly twinkle in his eye.

Heads swung round to see who it was got such a welcome from Albert Pierrepoint. As the group of about half a dozen parted to allow me to get to the bar, Pierrepoint said to one of the people closest to him, 'This is Syd Dernley – my new assistant.'

They were the magic words which guaranteed me a warm welcome there and a pleasant evening.

There were three of them working behind the bar: Pierrepoint, his wife Anne, and a barmaid. They were busy, and what conversation I had with him was in short snatches and of course nothing more than generalities.

I quickly saw that there were two distinct types of customer in the pub. There were the trippers who were not at all interested in the beer but were there to see Albert Pierrepoint the hangman. Then there were the regulars who lived nearby and who used The Struggler as their local; to them Albert was the landlord, and he was on first-name terms with most of them.

Not that Pierrepoint trusted even his cronies when it came to his official duties. The first time he left me to serve someone, he said, 'Don't tell 'em owt, Syd.' It was said with a laugh but there was just the hint of an edge which brought back memories of the other Pierrepoint. The group laughed too – but sounded me out all the same. 'Have you been his assistant for long?' asked one.

I was rescued by the bloke whom Pierrepoint had spoken to first when I came in and who was, I supposed, one of his friends. 'Hey, none of that,' he interrupted. 'You don't want to get the lad in trouble with his boss.'

I was relieved at the interruption and I thought to myself that they would have been most disappointed if I had answered the question truthfully and told them just how new and green I was!

Settled in with a pint and my new friends, I drank in the atmosphere of the place. The sightseers came and went. Some just sat with a drink and stared at Pierrepoint, talking to each other in whispers. Some asked to shake hands with him – which he invariably did with a friendly smile. There was even a point when two young women came up to the bar together and handed an autograph book over the bar. 'Can we 'ave your autograph, Mr Pierrepoint?' they asked.

'Course you can my loves,' he said with a big smile. They looked relieved that they had not been rebuffed, and they got the hangman's autograph.

That evening there was too, the first of many attempts to bribe me – and it came from one of Albert's cronies. He was a big fat man and there was a point when I found myself cut off from the rest of the group, talking to him.

'I'd really like to see an execution,' was his opening line.

I bet you would, I thought, but said nothing.

'Can you fix it for me?' he asked. 'Can you persuade Albert to let me come on a job?'

I was so astonished, I didn't say anything.

'Look,' he said in deadly earnest, 'I'll pay you twenty quid if you'll talk to him and get him to take me along.'

Bear in mind that an assistant executioner's fees were three guineas a time – so he was offering six times what I would get at an execution. It was also more than a fortnight's pay at the pit.

'What do you say?'

He clearly did not have a clue what an execution was like. He obviously thought that there were so many people around the scaffold that one more would not even be noticed!

'Twenty quid,' he repeated earnestly.

For an instant, I had a picture of the scene in the condemned cell: governor, under-sheriff, engineer officer … and this fat man jammed in a corner trying to look insignificant. It was such a funny thought, I cracked out laughing. His face fell.

'Look, I'm sorry,' I told him, 'but even if I wanted to, it just isn't possible.'

He looked crestfallen. 'Sorry,' he said. 'I just thought I'd ask.'

I smiled politely and he disappeared to the other side of the group.

It was almost nine o'clock, the pub was packed and Pierrepoint was working flat out. I caught his eye and he came over. 'I'm heading home now,' I told him. 'Can I buy you a drink before I go?'

'No thanks,' said Pierrepoint with a smile. 'Look here,' and he nodded down behind the bar. I leaned over. There were sixteen half-pint glasses of beer in a row.

'Everybody wants to buy me a drink,' he explained.

The whole lot were drinks which the sightseers had paid for, so that when they got home they could tell their friends they had bought the hangman a drink. Pierrepoint said 'Cheers', took a sip from one and put it down behind the bar.

'What'll you do with them?' I asked him.

'Sell 'em, of course,' said Pierrepoint with a laugh.

'In that case, I will not buy you a drink! Goodnight Albert.'

'Goodnight Syd. See you soon,' he replied.

As the trolley-bus rolled back into Manchester, I wondered how soon.

I joined Belle Vue excursions several times over the next few months so that I could go to The Struggler, but the summer came and went with no further communication from the Prison Commissioners. I followed each murder case reported in the newspapers, wondering if this could be the one, but the call did not come, and I was beginning to worry that I had been blacklisted because of my cheek in writing to the Commissioners asking for expenses.

The waiting finally ended on Friday 23rd September. I had been working on the night shift and was just about to go to bed when the postman delivered the letter. I ripped the envelope open.

'I have a condemned prisoner in my custody and you have been recommended to me by the Prison Commissioners for employment as assistant executioner.

Two copies are enclosed of the Memorandum of Conditions to which any person acting as Assistant Executioner is required to conform, and if you are willing to act as Assistant Executioner I should be glad if you would sign and return one copy of the Memorandum to me in the enclosed stamped addressed envelope. I would be obliged if you would treat the matter as urgent.

The date of the execution has been fixed provisionally for the 11th October but if the woman appeals ...'

My heart stopped ... if the *WOMAN* appeals!

I looked at the address. Holloway. Christ, they wanted me to help hang a woman!

I looked at the thin sheet of paper in utter disbelief. What was I going to do?

The letter, which was signed by the Chief Officer, E. Higgins, did not say who the condemned woman was but I knew without being told ... Margaret Laughlan Williams. She was young and pretty, and when she stabbed her husband to death three months after the wedding ceremony she made headline news.

It was a pathetic tale which emerged at the Old Bailey trial. The twenty-one-year-old WRAC had met her husband, Squadron Sergeant Major Montague Williams, at Klagenfurt in Austria, where they had both been stationed with the army. Williams became besotted with her, even though he was fourteen years older, but what he did not know was that she was a lesbian. She turned down his proposals numerous times but one evening when she was drunk, he proposed again and she accepted. As soon as she sobered up she realized she had made a terrible mistake, but, afraid that she would ridicule him and blight his career if she backed out, and hoping marriage would stifle her lesbian tendencies, she decided to go through with it. Things were, though, spelled out to Williams. She did not yet love him, and she would not sleep with him until she could say she did love him. The infatuated man agreed to her condition and the strange wedding ceremony with the secret clause took place at Torpichen in Scotland.

The marriage was a disaster and after a stormy and drunken weekend, she stabbed him twice, once through the heart. She claimed she had retaliated after he started slapping her face and knocking her about.

Now I was being invited to help hang her. I stood with the letter in my hand and read it again … a woman! I had never even thought about having to hang a woman. During our training we had always talked – and I had always thought – of the condemned person as a man. In an idle moment someone had asked Hughes. Not having ever seen a woman executed, all he could say was that it was the same but he understood the tension was always greater and there was an attempt to make things even smoother and quicker. That was the only time it was mentioned.

I felt pretty uncomfortable about the prospect, but I wrote accepting the job. Eight days later I had a second letter from Holloway. Mrs Williams had been reprieved. I was relieved; with her being a young and pretty girl, there would undoubtedly have been a hell of a public outcry. I found out later that I need not have worried. Pierrepoint told me that he had been invited to hang Mrs Williams; he had accepted the appointment but he had not even bothered to make any arrangements to be away from the pub … it never looked a starter to him!

I did not have to wait long for the next invitation; just four weeks. This time the letter was from the governor at Durham Prison and I had no qualms at all about accepting. The job was to hang a nasty piece of work, a shipyard worker from South Shields who had strangled his wife when she refused to get out of bed to attend to their crying child. It looked a pretty black-and-white affair to me. I could not believe it when he was reprieved!

I was beginning to wonder if I would ever get started and with my training now almost a year past, I was beginning to worry about what would happen when I did get a job. I wrote to Albert and he was reassuring. 'I see you have been unlucky on one or two of your jobs but that's how they go, it will change round before long.'

Pierrepoint was right; even as he wrote that weekend, events which were to make it 'change round' were already taking place in two northern mining villages only fifteen miles apart. The first

murder came on the Saturday night when a miner killed a
seaman's wife he had been drinking with. Her body was found
in a field … she had been bashed about, her clothing ripped, she
had been sexually assaulted and finally strangled with her own
scarf. Detectives said it looked as if she had been attacked by a
wild animal. The miner's explanation was that when he
suggested they make love she had asked for ten shillings.

Even as the police were grilling him on the Sunday, news
came in of a second murder. Another young miner had killed a
lass he had known since childhood. This was a crime of passion;
he loved the girl but she preferred his friend. He had shot her
but bungled his own suicide attempt and ended up in hospital,
where they were to patch him up so that he could be hanged.

The two men were tried at the same assizes and it was
decided that they would hang together, a fairly rare event at
Durham. The Prison Commissioners invited me to assist at the
execution of the lover. Without hesitation, I replied accepting
the engagement, at the same time dashing off a letter to
Pierrepoint to let him know I had finally got a job and to find out
if he was going to be the number one. I felt a little uneasy when I
received his reply a couple of days later; he was going to be in
Germany dealing with some Nazi war criminals. Steve Wade
was to be in charge at Durham. Pierrepoint assured me, 'You'll
find him a nice chap.'

For no reason that I could explain, my sense of unease grew
as the date of the execution approached. I never regarded myself
as being in the slightest clairvoyant or prophetic, but a sixth
sense warned me that it was not going to be straightforward. I
told myself that I was being stupid, that it was just nerves, that I
was worried about my first job, that I was anxious about working
with Wade whom I had never met; but though I could never
explain it, I knew there was going to be trouble.

I was in a sombre mood as I set out for Durham on Monday
12th December, twenty-four hours before the execution was
scheduled to take place. Premonitions apart, I was very
conscious of the fact that I was set on a course which would
change my life irrevocably. Today I was just an ordinary pit
welder, tomorrow I would be a hangman. I was also worried
about how I would perform, since it was now a year since I had
attended the training week at Pentonville. I would have been
terrified if I had known what had happened to George

Dickinson a few weeks earlier – but that was a secret Pierrepoint kept from me for more than a year.

Fortunately things began to brighten up as I changed trains at Sheffield. 'Syd!' someone shouted out.

I would have known that Birmingham voice anywhere – Harry Allen! I turned round to see him striding along the platform towards me. 'Can't I go anywhere without you!' I laughed as we shook hands.

'You've got to have somebody to look after you,' he retorted with one of those familiar grins.

It was the best thing that could have happened. Instead of a lonely trip with the tension building up, we talked our heads off and it was quite impossible to be serious with Harry for very long. We found an empty compartment and I discovered that Harry had been engaged as an assistant for "the animal".

'Have you done a job yet?' he asked.

'No,' I replied. 'How about you?'

'Had a few invitations – but they were all reprieved,' said Harry. 'Then to get a double first job! I don't suppose they have many doubles here.'

'That's good,' I told him. 'They'll be so bloody nervous themselves, they won't be watching us so carefully!'

Harry laughed. 'The screws may be nervous – but Albert Pierrepoint won't be.'

'He's not on the job,' I told him, trying not to sound too smug. 'Steve Wade's the number one.'

Harry looked suitably impressed by my inside knowledge and I had to tell him about my trips to The Struggler and about getting to know Pierrepoint and his cronies.

The journey was passing off pleasantly until Harry had one of his flashes of inspiration, soon after we had passed through Doncaster. 'Steve Wade lives near here!' he announced. I looked at him expectantly.

'I wonder if he's on the train?' he continued.

I could tell by the look on his face that something was going on in his mind. 'So?'

'Well, let's see if we can spot him,' said Harry enthusiastically.

'Do you know what he looks like?' I asked.

'No idea,' said Harry cheerfully.

'Well that's that,' I said, thinking the subject closed.

Harry was not to be put off so easily. 'Look, we know he's a bookie – should be able to spot him easily. Let's take a look.'

I was less than enthusiastic about the idea but I did not mind stretching my legs, so off we went along the train looking in the compartments to see if we could spot someone who looked like a bookie – and a hangman.

We had only travelled along two carriages when it looked as if Harry's hunch had paid off. In one of the compartments was a big man with a florid complexion and a loud checked sports jacket. He was reading the sports pages of a newspaper.

'Got to be him!' said Harry triumphantly.

I had to agree that he certainly did look like a bookie.

'Shall I speak to him?' asked Harry.

'No' I urged. 'Even if it is him, he wouldn't be pleased.'

The man in the carriage heard us talking and looked up. Harry smiled and nodded but the man ignored him and turned back to his newspaper.

'I'm going to speak to him,' said Harry, making up his mind.

'If you do, I'm off,' I warned him, and as he opened the compartment door I fled back to our own carriage.

I scarcely had time to sit down before Harry rushed in breathlessly, laughing his head off.

'What happened?' I asked, 'Was it him?'

'No,' laughed Harry. 'I asked him if he was Steve. He said he wasn't so I got the hell out of it.'

I thought about clause six of the memorandum of conditions for assistant executioners: 'He should avoid attracting public attention in going to or from the prison; he should clearly understand that his conduct and general behaviour must be respectable and discreet.'

Harry was sitting with a merry smile on his face. 'I wonder what he would have said if I'd asked him if he was the hangman?' he mused, and then burst out laughing again.

The rest of the journey passed off pleasantly and we arrived in Durham without further incident. It was the first time I had ever been to the city; I thought it a very quaint and pleasant place as we strolled through the centre to reach the prison. We arrived with half an hour to spare and I found to my astonishment that we were walking up to a building which looked more like a stately home than a gaol, built of stone with an imposing frontage and a country-house style clock on the roof.

In the gatehouse office, Harry Kirk was already waiting with another man in civilian clothes. The stranger was taller than me, about 5 feet 9 inches tall, and slim. He was wearing a charcoal grey suit. It was Steve Wade. He did not look anything like a bookie.

Wade was a quiet man and said nothing more than hello when Kirky did the introductions. Kirky was his usual cheery self and the screws were friendly enough, as you would expect. They did not often see hangmen and here they had a whole collection of them! We were taken to our quarters in the prison hospital to drop off our gear and then immediately we went to have a look at the condemned men.

The prison had a deserted and silent air about it. The corridors and landings had obviously been cleared to allow us to go about our business, for we saw no prisoners and only a handful of screws on the short journey to the condemned suite. Wade and one of the senior warders walked in front. They were two or three paces ahead of the rest of us when I saw the warder pass over a piece of paper which I assumed would have on it the condemned men's heights and weights. The screw also said something – and Wade suddenly halted in mid-stride. He turned and gave the man a searching look, but the screw just shrugged his shoulders and they continued walking. I had not been close enough to hear what had been said but it had certainly startled Wade. Was something wrong?

As we arrived outside the first of the condemned cells, one look at Wade's troubled face was enough to answer the question – something *was* wrong!

This cell contained 'the animal'.

Wade moved the peephole cover aside and looked. After a few moments, he had apparently seen enough for he stepped away and nodded at me. 'Have a look.'

Trying to look as if I had done it a dozen times before, I walked over and put my eye to the hole. I could see pretty well the whole of the inside of the cell, although it was not necessary because the man and the two warders on the death watch were sitting round the table playing cards. I had a side view of 'the animal'; he looked a big lad but the thing which surprised me most was that he seemed so young. It all looked normal enough to me … so what was wrong?

Harry was told to have a look and then we moved quietly on to the second condemned cell, which in this prison was not next to the first but a couple of paces away across the landing. Again Wade slid the spyhole cover aside and peered in, but now he took a long, long time. My stomach was churning as I waited to get my first sight of the man I was to help hang. Wade took his eye away from the peephole, blinked, and went back for another look. After what seemed an age, he stepped away and indicated that Kirky should look. The tension was almost unbearable as the seconds ticked away but then Kirky flicked the spyhole shut. I was about to step forward to the door when Wade turned on his heel and walked off to the execution chamber.

What the hell was going on? That something out of the ordinary was happening seemed very clear, and Wade was worried. The answer, whatever it was, lay in that second cell and I had not been invited to look, even though there was the man that I had been engaged for.

We stood around silently in the execution chamber, waiting for them to get the condemned men out of their cells. Hughes had told us they normally took them off to the chapel or the exercise yard so that the gallows could be rigged and tested without them being alerted to the fact that they were just half a dozen steps away from the scaffold. Wade, a pencil in hand, was looking at the paper and doing his calculations. A warder walked into the execution chamber and told Wade, 'It's clear now, you can go ahead.'

The next few minutes as we got to work were quite fascinating. It had obviously been agreed beforehand that Kirky would take a back seat to give Harry and me the chance to gain experience, for he spent the whole time leaning against the wall chatting to one of the screws. In contrast, Wade controlled and double-checked everything from the moment he opened the execution boxes and took out the three ropes. He examined each of them minutely before rejecting one of them which was immediately coiled up and returned to the box. He measured the drop along the rope and marked it with chalk. I was allowed to shackle the rope to one of the chains hanging down from the beam and I had to go up the steps to adjust the chain as we got the chalk mark to the height of the man's head, but he went up the steps to check both the shackling and the chain when I had finished.

Satisfied, the process was repeated on the other side of the gallows with Harry and, given our inexperience, in a surprisingly short time the sandbags were noosed and the whole apparatus ready for testing.

For a single execution the rope hangs from the beam in the middle of the trap; for a double hanging there are two brackets on either side of the centre point. The bags were standing three feet apart. Wade took a last look around and told the chief screw that he could get the governor.

We waited in silence until the official party arrived – prison governor, engineer officer and the under-sheriff of Durham. They looked grim as they trooped in and arranged themselves around the trap. Wade looked at the governor. 'Ready sir?' he asked quietly.

The governor nodded and Wade knocked off the safety devices and pushed the lever. The trapdoors crashed downwards and the sandbags plummeted into the pit. For a few seconds we all stared into the yawning hole, almost mesmerized by the sight of the taut rope and the bags now hanging below our feet. The governor looked at Wade.

'No problems?'

'No sir,' replied Wade.

We left the execution chamber on the heels of the official party. The door was locked behind us, the sandbags left hanging to take the stretch out of the ropes. We were back in our quarters about thirty minutes or so after we had quitted them.

The screw who was to spend the night with us said he would go and let them know we were ready for our tea. 'Take ten minutes,' said Wade, giving him a not-so-subtle hint that he wanted to talk to us in private.

Once he was out of the way, Wade told us to gather round and explained that there was indeed a problem with the lover. 'When he tried to kill himself, he injured his neck,' said Wade, leaning his head slightly over to the left to illustrate what he meant.

'We'll soon straighten it for him!' chipped in Kirky, mockingly.

Wade ignored the remark. 'They don't think it will make any difference, and I'm sure they're right. It's not much.'

Neither Harry nor I said a word and Wade carried on, 'This is the way we're going to do it. Syd will come with me to the first cell and get him. You, Kirky, will take Harry and get the other one.'

'Let me run through it,' he said, turning to me. 'When we get the signal from the governor, which may be nothing more than a slight nod, we go in nice and steady – we don't charge through the door. Once we've got his arms strapped, I'll lead the way and you follow on behind him. I want him on that trap in eight seconds flat. You strap his legs and get clear. Got that?'

'Right,' I replied.

'You two', he said, turning to Kirky and Harry, 'go in as soon as we start moving. I want your man on the trap as soon as I've got the noose on the first. You stop him on the mark, Kirky, and get out of the way. Harry, you get that strap on his legs as quick as you can because we'll all be waiting for you by then.'

Tea arrived a few minutes later; a good helping of bacon, egg and fried bread, with as much bread and butter as we could eat, and mugs of tea. It was a bright spot in what turned out to be a dull evening. Wade was a very staid character compared with Pierrepoint. Perhaps he was worried about the job, perhaps he was worried about having two new boys on the job; at any rate he was very reserved and said very little. Kirky did his best to keep the conversation going but it was nothing like so entertaining an evening as we had spent before Farrell's hanging, and in the end even he gave up.

By nine o'clock I would have loved to take a stroll in the prison grounds, or even stretch my legs in the corridors. I was finding it difficult not to keep glancing at my watch as the time slowly passed by, and impossible not to think of the two men in the condemned cells and what they were doing in these last few hours of their lives. I could not leave our quarters, of course. We were locked in for the night.

Eventually the time reached ten o'clock and it was a relief to climb into bed. I lay there for a while, running over in my mind how it should go in the morning, suffering the odd butterflies, but then I dropped off and I slept like a log.

I was still enjoying the warm blackness when something dragged me back to consciousness. For a moment as I opened my eyes I had no idea where I was, but there was the tame screw's face smiling as he shook my arm. 'It's seven-thirty,' he said as I struggled to gather my wits.

'Morning, sleepy head,' said Kirky cheerfully. 'I thought you were going to stay there all day.'

'Morning,' I replied, swinging my legs out of bed. All the

others were up and about.

The mood was serious as we washed, shaved and dressed. They brought us some mugs of tea at about quarter to eight. As we sipped the drink Wade said, 'Quiet's the word when we get back down there. They'll be in their cells, so no unnecessary noise.'

Quiet was the word as we headed down to the execution chamber. There was an eerie silence hanging over the place. All the prisoners were locked in their cells, all the peepholes covered over. The doors we passed through were opened and shut without any of the normal banging and rattling.

As we approached the condemned cells I saw that during the night coconut matting had been laid down along the corridor for a distance of about thirty feet from the condemned cells, so our approach was noiseless.

Inside the execution chamber we recovered the sandbags. Down in the drop Kirky, using a small pair of steps, eased the trapdoors off the retaining springs and they were hauled up so that Wade could re-set the lever. He then re-measured the drops marked on the ropes. In both cases the rope had stretched by about half an inch, so Harry and I had to go back up the steps to the beam and adjust the chains again until Wade was satisfied that the arrangements were perfect. The work was performed almost without a word being spoken, and there was only the odd clink or creak from the equipment which could not possibly have been heard outside the cell.

The last job was to tie the nooses at the right height. Wade gathered the loops of rope together and held them at the height he wanted. I tied the packthread round the loops. Wade repeated the process with Harry. The gallows was now ready, the two nooses hanging at just the right height to slip over the heads of the condemned men. We left as quietly as we had come.

The next forty-five minutes as we waited in our quarters for the call were about the worst in my life. Everything that needed to be said had been said and it was clearly no time for social chit-chat, so we sat there and waited. There was fear afoot in the prison; you could almost smell it. The whole place was silent, waiting.

The butterflies in my stomach, which had disappeared when we went to the execution chamber and had something to do, were back with a vengeance. A jumble of thoughts flitted through my mind. Questions: Would we do a good job? Would I put up a good showing? Would we be quick? There were fears too: Will he fight? How will I handle it if he does?

I looked at the people in the room. Strangely, as the time drew nearer, Wade looked less worried than he had done last night. Kirky, staring out of a barred window, looked as relaxed as could be. Harry looked as nervous as I felt and the screw looked positively awful – pale and drawn.

I heard Hughes' voice as clearly as if he was speaking into my ear: 'When you walk in, look firm and determined but not brutal – you don't want to panic him unnecessarily.'

I remembered another piece of his advice: 'When you get the tap, get off the trap or you go down with it – and it's a nasty drop even if you haven't got a rope round your neck!'

I looked at my watch … five minutes to nine. God, were we never to get moving?

The door opened and a warder took a step into the room. Wade got to his feet. 'It's time,' he said simply. 'Are you ready?' I nodded. I don't think I could have said anything. Kirky looked across at me and smiled. 'Make it a good job, young 'un,' he said quietly.

I followed Wade out of the door thinking that as I was his assistant, I'd better stick close to him. With a screw leading the way and Kirky and Harry following behind, we headed for the condemned cells. The timing was perfect because as we entered the wing we fell in just a couple of paces behind the official party.

In those last few moments I was most conscious of faces, faces turned towards us … screws standing quite still at strategic points, all staring at us … the people standing near the doors of the condemned cells watching us approach … the faces of the official party as they glanced over their shoulders … but above all the face of the clock hanging on the wall at the end of the wing. It was a gigantic thing, about three feet across, and the minute hand was now just a fraction away from nine o'clock.

We were halfway to the condemned cells when the silence was broken and my blood froze. The sound was faint to begin with but it rapidly swelled – singing!

I could not believe my ears. '*Jesu … lover … of my soul*,' croaked the quavering voice.

Another stronger voice joined in: '*Let me to thy bosom fly.*'

'Who the hell is that?' I asked one of the screws who was walking along beside me.

He looked shattered but he was not going to admit it. 'It's one of them you're going to top in a minute,' he replied, trying to sound cool.

With that eerie sound ringing round the wing, we arrived outside the condemned cells. The singing was coming from number two cell, and for the next thirty seconds we stood listening to the doomed man and his priest singing in harmony. In other circumstances it might have been lovely. Here, now, it was weird and unreal.

Everyone was in position as the hands of the huge clock moved the last fraction of an inch to nine o'clock: Wade and I outside the number one cell; Harry and Kirky a few steps away across the landing outside the number two cell; the governor, under-sheriff and engineer officer outside the door of the execution chamber itself.

The signal, when it came, was both nod and hand signal. Wade moved straight through the door and I followed him into the cell. It seemed quite crowded with the two warders backing clear and the white-faced priest sitting on the other side of the table looking up at us. The condemned man was positioned, as per the book, sitting at the table with his back to the door.

By the time I got to him, he was on his feet and Wade was bringing his left arm behind his back. There was no resistance as I caught hold of his right arm. He just let me bring it behind his back and Wade was waiting for it.

Things were moving incredibly quickly, there was hardly time to take anything in. Wade was walking through the yellow doors. Our man had turned to watch him but had not moved so I just put my hand on his shoulder and, with only the gentlest of pressure, he started to follow. A warder either side of him, we walked through and on to the trap. Wade stopped him and I slipped the legstrap out of my pocket, bobbed down and fastened it round his ankles. I doubt I had ever done it so quickly but by the time I stood up and took a pace off the trap, Wade had finished and the man was standing with his head hidden under the bag and the noose round his neck.

I looked round to make sure I was not in the way of Kirky and his man whom I expected would be just a pace or two away by now. They were not there!

The shock was enormous. I could not believe my eyes. They should have been on the trap by now and there was no sign of them!

They were having some sort of trouble, but what? As the seconds ticked away, I strained to hear what was going on, but there was not a sound coming from the other side of the landing. That at least was reassuring because whatever was going wrong it was not some massive fight. We would have heard that.

I looked around the cell. Wade was staring through the open door, brow creased in a frown, with wide, worried eyes. By God, he looked worried. The governor and the under-sheriff looked as white as a pair of sheets.

In the centre of all this, the hooded and noosed figure of our man – who should have been dead by now – stood waiting patiently without a sound.

I looked back through the door. Still nothing. I felt so helpless; I wanted to run through and help or do something, but I knew I had to stand just where I was.

A double hanging should take around fifteen seconds from start to finish; we had now been standing with our man ready to go for at least forty-five seconds, although it felt like hours.

A sound to my right brought my eyes back from the door into the execution chamber. One of the screws seemed about to take a pace towards our man, a look almost of horror on his face. The hooded figure was starting to sway. He was going to faint!

At that moment Kirky rushed through the door followed by the lover and Harry. Kirky, looking red-faced and flustered, immediately peeled off to the left and Wade in a blur of motion was stopping the man on the chalk T. In what seemed almost one motion, he whipped the white hood over the man's head and flicked the noose on. I didn't even see Harry get the legstrap on before Wade was hurling himself off the trap. The lever went over and away the whole lot went with that massive boom.

The two men went down and stopped. That was it, they were dead.

Kirky went over to the little trapdoor in the corner and went down into the drop. By the time he had got the small steps in position so he could reach the bodies, he had been joined by the doctor who had suddenly appeared. A couple of buttons flew off as he ripped open the shirt of the first man. As the doctor went up and held a stethoscope to the chest of the corpse, I noticed that its toes were pointing straight down to the floor. The hooded head was lolling slightly to the side because of the broken neck. Having confirmed that one was dead, the process was repeated on the second man.

While this was going on, I confess that my legs felt a little shaky, not because of the execution but because of the near catastrophe. The two men had died cleanly but by God it had come close to being a shambles. Another few seconds and our man would have collapsed, of that there was no doubt. What had gone wrong?

In the execution chamber nothing was said, although it was quite obvious from the look on Wade's face that quite a lot was going to be said. Everyone filed out of the chamber and the doors were locked so that the two men would hang for the customary hour … even though they were already dead.

As soon as we arrived back in our quarters they served breakfast. The tame screw was there, so still nothing was said, although there was an atmosphere that you could have cut with a knife. As soon as the meal was over, Wade and Kirk disappeared with the tame screw, leaving Harry and me alone. The door had scarcely closed when I turned to Harry. 'What happened?'

'The bugger just didn't want to go,' said Harry quietly. 'He just wasn't ready. You heard the singing?'

I nodded.

'Well I can tell you it was bloody weird walking into that condemned cell. Him and the priest were still singing when we got up to him. It was only when Kirky got hold of his arm that they stopped and I reckon they'd have carried on then if they could have done.'

The experience had clearly shaken Harry, and I was pleased – selfishly I suppose, – that I had been switched.

'He just wouldn't bring his arm up for Kirky', Harry continued, 'and until he got the strap on I couldn't do anything with the other one. The priest was standing there in a state of shock. It was pretty awful.'

'What did you do?' I asked, imagining the scene.

'In the end we just had to force him,' said Harry. 'It wasn't that difficult. He wasn't a particularly strong bloke.'

'What a job to get first time,' I said.

'Did we seem to be a very long time?' asked Harry.

'Dead right you did,' I replied with feeling. 'I thought you were never going to bloody well come. Our man was a couple of seconds away from passing out. I reckon he was standing on the trap ready to go for close on a minute. It was getting too much for him and he was starting to sway.'

'Blimey,' said Harry, his eyes widening.

At ten o'clock we returned to the execution chamber, took the bodies down and packed the equipment away in the boxes. Wade went off to write his report, which must have been interesting, and we got paid – or rather half paid. They gave us £1 11s 6d, half the three guineas fee for an assistant executioner, with the rest to follow later; a method of payment from the days when hangmen with a jingle in their pockets were likely to leave the jail, get boozed up and start blabbing their mouths off.

Harry and I travelled back together as far as Sheffield. When we parted he was still a bit down in the mouth, worried that a black mark had gone on his record already. For my part, it was only on the last leg of the journey to Mansfield Woodhouse, left alone with my thoughts, that it began to sink in that now I really was a hangman. I found it hard to make up my mind how I felt about it. I did not have a feeling of excitement or exaltation. Probably my strongest emotion was one of relief and satisfaction that I had got through the experience without disgracing myself.

5   The Innocent Man

The great nightmare for any law-abiding country which operates the death penalty is that a mistake could be made and an innocent man or woman be put to death. Many people believe the nightmare became reality at Pentonville Prison on a March morning in 1950 when Albert Pierrepoint and I hanged a twenty-five-year-old lorry-driver called Timothy John Evans. What is quite certain is that there was later sufficient doubt for Evans to be given a posthumous free pardon, the only executed criminal ever to be pardoned in Britain.

No-one could have imagined the incredible events which were to ensue when Evans walked into the police station at Merthyr Tydfil in Wales on a November afternoon and said that he had come to give himself up. Evans was born in Wales but he lived in London from the age of eleven. He was married to a twenty-year-old London girl, Beryl, and they lived with their fourteen-month-old baby daughter in a flat on the second floor of a house at 10 Rillington Place.

He told a detective constable, 'I have disposed of my wife. I put her down a drain. I cannot sleep and I want to get it off my chest.'

In the next few days the lorry-driver was to give several different versions of what happened to his wife, and how she ended up dead. Sitting in the Welsh police station he spun a fantastic tale of how she had died trying to end an unwanted pregnancy. He claimed that a stranger he met at a transport cafe on the road between Ipswich and Colchester had given him a bottle containing liquid which he said would get rid of the baby. Evans told the police that he was not very happy about it but his wife had found the bottle when she went into his coat pocket for a cigarette.

The following evening he arrived home and found her dead

in bed. Evans said that after spending half the night trying to make up his mind what to do, he eventually decided to get rid of the body. In the early hours of the morning he got her downstairs and after checking that the coast was clear, raised the manhole cover in the street outside the house and pushed her in head first. He quit his job, sold the furniture and left London. He had been staying with his aunt in Wales for the past two weeks.

Evans was put on ice in the cells and a report was telephoned to the police in London. That evening a squad of officers was despatched to Rillington Place where it rapidly became obvious that Evans was lying. It took three policemen to raise the manhole cover, which the slightly built Evans said he had lifted on his own in the middle of the night. When they got the cover off they found the drain was empty. There was no body.

The squad packed up and returned to their station; news of the fruitless search was flashed back to Merthyr Tydfil. At nine o'clock in the evening Evans was questioned again. There was no body in the drain, he was told. For a few minutes he continued to maintain that he had put it there, but then he abruptly changed his story, admitted that he had been lying and gave a new version of events.

He now claimed that Reg Christie, the man who lived in the ground-floor flat at 10 Rillington Place, had offered to help get rid of the baby. Christie said he had been training to be doctor before the war and could get rid of it without any trouble at all. Evans said he did not want it to happen but his wife went ahead and made the arrangements. When he got home from work on Tuesday afternoon, Christie was waiting for him. 'It's bad news,' he said. 'It didn't work.'

Beryl's body was lying on the bed, beneath an eiderdown. When he pulled the cover back, Evans could see that she had been bleeding from the mouth and nose and between the legs. Christie said her stomach had been 'septic poisoned' and she had died in the middle of the afternoon.

Christie took Evans into the kitchen and then disappeared for about fifteen minutes. When he came back he said he had put the body in an empty flat on the first floor and would dispose of it down the drains later in the night. Evans claimed he had protested but Christie said it was the only thing he could do or he would be in trouble with the police.

Later Christie had arranged for the baby, Geraldine, to go to a couple in East Acton and Christie had advised Evans to leave his job and get out of London.

At one o'clock in the morning, details of the new story were telephoned to the Notting Hill police station and officers went round and knocked up Evans' mother, Mrs Agnes Probert, who lived a short distance from Rillington Place. She was able to confirm one thing: Beryl Evans and the baby had disappeared.

Soon after daylight another squad of police was despatched to Rillington Place to check the flat vacated by Evans. They found nothing, but the decision was made to send two detectives to Wales to bring Evans back to London. The following day more men were sent to the house, this time determined to take the place apart if necessary. As the search of the building progressed, an officer opened the door of the old wash-house and found it stacked with wood, old floorboards which had recently been taken up in the house. He moved some of the planks and found a large parcel, wrapped up in a green tablecloth and tied with old cord, jammed under the wash-house sink. The missing Beryl Evans had been found. A moment later the policeman discovered a second, smaller, parcel ... the body of baby Geraldine. Both had been strangled, the baby with a tie which was still so tightly round the neck that it later had to be cut off.

Evans was brought back to London, unaware that the bodies of his wife and child had been found. In an office at the Notting Hill police station a chief inspector called Jennings faced him with the news: both Beryl and Geraldine had been found and they had both been strangled. 'I have reason to believe that you were responsible for their deaths,' Jennings added.

If Evans was innocent, something quite extraordinary then happened. He simply answered, 'Yes.' A few moments later he made a complete confession.

'She was incurring one debt after another and I could not stand it any longer so I strangled her with a piece of rope and took her down to the flat below the same night ... I waited till the Christies downstairs had gone to bed, then I took her to the wash-house after midnight. This was on Tuesday 8th November. On Thursday evening after I came home from work I strangled my baby in our bedroom with my tie and later that night I took her down into the wash-house after the Christies had gone to bed.'

Then the man who had all but signed his own death warrant

told the detectives, 'It's a great relief to get it off my chest. I feel better already.'

Evans was charged with murdering both his wife and baby daughter although, following the usual practice of the time, when he went on trial at the Old Bailey he faced just one capital charge. The prosecution elected to proceed on the count of murdering baby Geraldine. The man who had given three entirely different versions of what happened, and a full confession, now pleaded not guilty and reverted to account number two: Christie was the killer.

Christie, a balding ledger clerk, came over well in the witness box. He refuted everything Evans said. He had not suggested that he could end Mrs Evans' pregnancy; he had not said he was training to be a doctor before the war; he did not know anything about the deaths of Beryl and Geraldine Evans; he did not move Beryl's body to the empty flat.

Evans was taken apart under cross-examination. He had to admit he was a liar who had given false stories to the police. When he was asked why he had confessed, he said that he was frightened the detectives would take him downstairs and start kicking him about. When he was asked why Christie should have strangled his wife, he could give no reason.

The jury gave his claims short shrift. It took them just thirty-five minutes to reach their decision, and eight weeks later, on 10th March, Pierrepoint and I went to work at Pentonville. With the young strangler safely in his unmarked prison grave, that seemed to be the end of the matter. Most people quickly forgot the name Timothy John Evans.

So it remained until another March day, three years later, when Berresford Brown, a new tenant at 10 Rillington Place, was having a nose round the flat which had recently been quitted by Reginald Christie. In the kitchen, he put his eye to a hole in the door of the old coal cupboard, which was now sealed off and papered over. After a moment, when his eye had adjusted to the gloom, he found himself looking at a woman's legs.

It was horrific. There were rotting corpses all over 10 Rillington Place. The bodies of three women were found in the cupboard; all had been strangled. Christie's wife, Ethel, was found buried under the floorboards in the front room; she too had been strangled. When the police dug up the garden they found the remains of two more women. Christie, who had been described at the trial of Evans as 'a perfectly innocent man', was a mass killer who had been slaughtering women for years. Most ominous of all, from the point of view of the Evans case, was the chilling fact that four of the women had been strangled and tied up in blankets … just like Mrs Evans and baby Geraldine.

Investigation was to show that Christie's murderous career had spanned at a least a decade. The skeletons in the garden were the remains of two women, Ruth Fuerst and Muriel Eady, whom Christie had killed during the war. He had finished with an orgy of slaughter: his wife in December 1952; two of the cupboard women, Rita Nelson and Kathleen Maloney, the following month, and Hectorina MacLennan a few weeks later. The monster had sexually abused all of the women, with the exception of his wife, as they died … or lay dead.

The question was, had he indulged his filthy lust in 1949? If he had murdered Beryl and Geraldine Evans, then we had hanged an innocent man. A week after Christie first appeared in court, the Home Secretary issued a licence for the bodies of Mrs Evans and her daughter to be exhumed from the grave in the Kensington Borough Cemetery where they had lain since 1949. The coffin, in which both mother and child had been buried, was raised early one May morning in the presence of three Home Office pathologists. It was taken to the local mortuary where the doctors had the grim task of carrying out another examination. Perhaps not surprisingly, it was to shed little new light on the happenings at Rillington Place.

Christie, on the other hand, was supplying new information. He confessed to his lawyer that he had strangled Beryl Evans. He said he convinced Timothy Evans that she had committed suicide by gassing herself and then deliberately frightened the lorry-driver by telling him that he would be suspected of having killed her because of the rows and fights they had.

At his trial, Christie claimed to have only a hazy recollection of those crimes and killings that it was impossible for him to deny. Strangely, though, he was quite clear and certain about one thing; he had not carried out the cold-blooded strangling of baby Geraldine. That was, of course, the crime for which Timothy Evans had been tried and hanged.

Astonishingly, the mass killer was believed. The Attorney-General, Sir Lionel Heald, who was leading for the prosecution in the case, even spoke in Christie's defence on that point when he made his closing speech to the jury. He said, 'Evans was convicted and executed for the murder of his child. No suggestion has been made, and there is not the slightest reason for anyone to think for a moment, that there is any question that Christie killed that child. There is enough on Christie without having it put on him as well.'

The Attorney-General may have believed that there was not the slightest reason for thinking that this man who had confessed to seven murders might also be guilty of strangling a baby, but few other people were so confident. Christie was sentenced to death on Thursday 25th June. There was uproar as the questions and the concern – which had been held back during the Christie trial – flooded forth. Within twenty-four hours there were calls for a public inquiry into the Evans case. On the floor of the House of Commons there was a barrage of questions aimed at Sir Maxwell Fyfe, the Home Secretary. Finally, on 6th July, just nine days before Christie was to hang, Sir Maxwell announced that the Recorder of Portsmouth, John Scott Henderson, was to carry out an inquiry into the Evans case.

Scott Henderson started work two days later; like almost everybody else, he was unaware that there had been a startling new development. Christie, resident in the very same condemned cell at Pentonville Prison where Evans had been held, was now not only denying that he had murdered baby Geraldine, he was also retracting his confession that he had killed Beryl Evans. The defence at his trial had been insanity, and he claimed that he had become confused in the interviews with his solicitor before the trial and had got the idea that it was necessary for him to confess to murders, the more the merrier.

Scott Henderson and his inquiry team interviewed Christie at Pentonville Prison. The mass killer was vague and rambling and seemed to be living in his own fuzzy dream world. He still denied murdering the baby but when he was questioned about the death of Mrs Evans he claimed that he could not remember and wanted to know the truth as much as anyone!

Scott Henderson delivered his report on Tuesday 14th July, the very eve of Christie's execution. His conclusions were, first, that the case against Evans at his trial was overwhelming. Second, there could be no doubt that Evans was responsible for the deaths of both Mrs Evans and baby Geraldine. Third,

Christie's statements, that he was responsible for the death of Mrs Evans, were not only unreliable but were untrue. His view was that Christie had come to the conclusions that it would be helpful with his defence of insanity if he confessed to the murder of Mrs Evans. Scott Henderson said that in his opinion there had been no miscarriage of justice in the Evans case.

The report produced pandemonium in the House of Commons. In some quarters it was greeted with utter disbelief. There was talk of prejudice, bias, concealment and suppression of evidence. On the floor of the House there were calls for an emergency debate and, when that was rejected, Opposition members tabled a motion calling for the report to be rejected and a high-powered select committee to be set up.

As the hours to Christie's execution slid away, there was a determined attempt to have the hanging delayed. One member, roared on by his colleagues, demanded that they have the chance to discuss the report before Christie had his mouth silenced for ever. Even as the battles were being fought at Westminster, Pierrepoint and his assistant were at the gaol preparing; regrettably I was not involved.

The mouth of the vital witness was closed for ever at a few seconds past nine o'clock the next morning. Pierrepoint told me that the strangler was pathetically co-operative.

The hanging of Christie was not, though, to be the end of the matter. The Timothy Evans affair would not go away. As the years passed there was no let-up in the stream of books, articles, questions in parliament and demands for new inquiries. The Conservative administration steadfastly refused to re-open the case, but in 1964, thirteen years of Tory rule came to an end when Harold Wilson led the Labour Party to victory in a general election. The following year, after all-party pressure, the new Home Secretary, Sir Frank Soskice, announced there would be a new inquiry. It would be independent and held in public, in a determined attempt to end the controversy once and for all. The job of heading it was given to Mr Justice Brabin, a fifty-two-year-old High Court Judge.

The Brabin Inquiry was in session for a total of thirty-two days and heard seventy-nine witnesses. Its report was published in October 1966 and caused a sensation. Brabin's conclusion was that Evans *was* a murderer ... but he was probably hanged for the wrong killing!

Brabin said that he did not believe that Evans had murdered Baby Geraldine, the crime for which he was tried and executed. He did think that Evans had murdered his wife, a crime which Christie had admitted. Explaining his thinking, the judge said that Evans and his wife had been unhappy together for some months. It was known that Evans had a violent temper and had struck his wife in rows. It would not be surprising if he used force on her again. At some point Christie became aware of Beryl's death and may have helped Evans because he did not want the police on the premises; he knew how shallow were the graves of his victims buried in the garden.

Mr Justice Brabin thought the murders were separate killings committed for different reasons: Beryl in anger; Geraldine because she was in the way. He did not believe that Evans killed the baby. 'I think it was more probably that Christie did it. It was a killing in cold blood which Christie would be more likely to do.'

At the end of it all, though, the judge admitted, it was now impossible to come to a conclusion on the guilt or innocence of Evans beyond reasonable doubt in either case.

Two weeks later it was announced that the Queen, on the Home Secretary's recommendation, had granted Timothy John Evans a posthumous free pardon. The Home Secretary told cheering Members of Parliament: 'In all the circumstances I do not think it would be right to allow Evans' conviction to stand. This case has no precedent and, I hope and believe, no successor.'

So there it was. Timothy John Evans had become the first executed criminal ever to be pardoned. We had – officially – hanged an innocent man.

So was Evans innocent? No-one asked Pierrepoint or myself, which was perhaps not surprising; evidence from hangmen would carry little weight with judges and lawyers and Members of Parliament. Yet if a man does not reveal the truth about himself in the moments before he goes to his death, when *will* he tell the truth? If the world of nightmares had become reality, if a man was being executed for a crime of which he was guiltless, surely he would protest, surely he would scream his innocence with his final breath …

The execution of Timothy Evans took place on Thursday

morning, 10th March 1950. I remember it very clearly because it was the first time that I worked with the Master, Albert Pierrepoint.

I travelled down to London the day before the execution and I was at Pentonville at about twenty minutes to four, in time to see Pierrepoint's entrance. The reception they gave him was amazing; everyone seemed to know him and to everyone he was 'Albert'. I lost count of the number of times I heard 'Afternoon Albert' as we passed screws and prison personnel. For his part, the man was in the most genial of moods, nodding and smiling to acknowledge the greetings.

There was not a trace of tension about Pierrepoint as we went to get our first look at Timothy John Evans. Pierrepoint peered through the peephole in the condemned cell door for a long time and then, satisfied, he moved away and nodded at me to take a look. I had a fairly quick glimpse but I will never forget it. The tiny Evans was dwarfed by the two screws on condemned cell duty. He was very, very thin and his face was showing the strain. It was like looking at an old man's head on a schoolboy's body.

We moved into the execution chamber and Pierrepoint smiled. 'He'll be out for a walk in a minute', he said, 'and then we can get to work.'

'He looks very small,' I ventured.

Pierrepoint looked up from the sheet of paper he was studying. 'Aye, we're going to give him a big drop,' he said, laconically. 'About eight foot I guess.'

In fact there was no guessing about it. Eight feet was exactly the drop he had decided to give Evans and it was a very long one.

The gallows worked perfectly when we tested them a quarter of an hour later and, with the sandbag dangling on the end of the rope, we went off to have our tea. Pierrepoint was quite incredible. He had an air of professionalism and assurance about him that I never saw equalled by any other hangman and it gave confidence to everyone else involved in the process, including me. That evening I felt none of the the fears I had at Durham, even though I was conscious of the fact that in the morning I would be watched much more carefully, given there were just two of us doing this job.

Pierrepoint was in good form and kept me and the tame screw

highly entertained. A few weeks earlier I had bought a box of books at an auction and the lot included three volumes on licensed houses and their management which I thought he might be interested in.

'Do you want to buy them?' I asked. 'They're all about keeping beer.'

'Three books on keeping beer,' he laughed. 'No thanks – I could do with three books on selling the bugger!'

We laughed.

'Anyway, talking of beer …' he said, with a meaningful look at the screw.

The man took the hint and broke out our ration of two bottles each. Pierrepoint and I settled down to the serious business of the evening, dominoes, fives and threes. He won, but we were not playing for money. The scene could have been a social evening anywhere in the land, apart from the spartan surroundings, the limited quantity of beer … and Timothy John Evans just a short distance away in the condemned cell, where the light was burning through the night for the last time.

They woke us at seven o'clock the next morning and after a wash and shave we went down to the execution chamber to re-set the equipment. During the night the rope had stretched by about half an inch; it always stretched by about half an inch but the measuring was always done again and the chains adjusted so that the felon got exactly the drop that the executioner had decided on the previous evening.

Pierrepoint by this time had hanged hundreds of people and at first there did not appear to be any trace of execution morning nerves. There was about him an air of grim determination but, although it was well hidden, even he was not immune to the tension, and he snapped at me in a quite ratty and unexpected way. We had almost finished re-rigging and he was holding up the coils of rope for me to tie with packthread, so that the noose would be at just the right height for Evans. Pierrepoint wanted the knot done in a particular way and, for a moment, I was all fingers and thumbs. 'Oh for God's sake, tie the bloody thing properly!' he snapped. Luckily I got the thing right next try and that was the end of the incident.

We had a leisurely breakfast, little being said, and then readied ourselves. Pierrepoint carefully folded the linen hood and placed it in his breast pocket, adjusting it until he felt it was just right. He had a last check of the armstrap, folded it in the S shape and put it in his jacket pocket. I watched him, the butterflies in my stomach multiplying as the time for the execution drew nearer.

With nothing left to fiddle with, we just sat there, waiting, in the silent prison. Then, with only a few moments to go, Pierrepoint did something quite extraordinary. He reached into his bag and brought out a packet of cigars. The screw and I watched in disbelief as he carefully selected one and lit it. He smoked for perhaps a minute, no more, before they came for us. Pierrepoint stood up and rested the cigar, still burning, on an ashtray. He then walked through the door on his way to the execution.

We arrived outside the condemned cell with less than a minute to spare; it might seem to be cutting it a bit fine but it was all part of the well worked-out strategy. It meant there was no crowd of people lurking outside the cell, making a noise which would alarm the condemned man. It also meant that we were not standing around for minutes on end in that highly-charged atmosphere.

When the signal came, a warder, standing ready at the condemned cell door, swung the key almost silently in the well-oiled lock. The screw pushed the door open and stood clear. I went in a pace behind Pierrepoint and drew abreast of him in the cell. Evans was sitting with his back to us and, by chance, happened to turn and look over his right shoulder. He looked straight into my eyes and started with fear. The expression was so desperate that I hesitated for a fraction of a second; for the first time in my life I was looking directly at a truly terrified man. Then, in the moment that our eyes were locked, he crumbled. His expression became one of resignation, all hope gone.

Pierrepoint reached him and I forced myself on. For a second Evans just sat there and made no move to rise; he was not resisting, just plain terrified. As we stood by him he slowly got to his feet. We strapped his arms and, significantly in the light of later developments, he said nothing and gave no indication that he wanted to speak. One of the guards motioned him to follow Pierrepoint and we went through into the execution chamber.

Once he was stationery on the trap, I got down, whipped the strap smoothly round his legs and immediately got clear. As I reached safety, Pierrepoint went for the lever. The floor disappeared and the small figure went down. I heard the rope break his neck. It was a sharp click; not a loud sound but very distinctive. That was the only time I ever heard the noise; normally the boom of the trapdoors drowned out everything else. The click was all there was ... Timothy John Evans was dead.

The doctor carried out his check and we returned to our quarters. Pierrepoint walked over to the ashtray and picked up his cigar. He drew on it and then slowly blew out a stream of smoke. It was still alight!

I was impressed, as it was intended I should be. It was a little trick that I was to see him repeat many times, a boast about himself and his nerve and his speed; although we had not been that quick with Evans. It had taken fifteen seconds, which was a long time for a single execution, at least by Pierrepoint's standards. There had not been any special problem, it was just that Evans had been so frightened and slow-moving. Pierrepoint said nothing about it as he enjoyed the cigar which he had started to smoke before the execution.

I never gave Evans another thought until the Christie story hit the front pages three years later and the full horror of the happenings at 10 Rillington Place became apparent. I felt numb as I read those first reports. Surely to God it was impossible that two stranglers lived in the same house ... and that meant we had hanged an innocent man!

I worried about it for some days and, to be brutally truthful, it was for Pierrepoint and me that I was concerned, not for Evans. For a time, I was afraid that any hour might bring reporters to my door; expecting that any day would bring stories in the papers about the hangmen who had executed an innocent man. When the newsmen did not arrive, I breathed a little easier and about a week after Christie's arrest I came up with a pretext to telephone Pierrepoint.

After a couple of minutes I asked him, 'What about Evans then?'

Instantly Pierrepoint replied, 'Well it's a bit too late to bother about him. There's nowt they can do about him now – is there?'

'No,' I replied, 'but I must say I'm a bit concerned about it.'

'Don't worry,' he said, 'they can't do anything to you.'

He sounded thoroughly cheesed off and I guessed that he had

been pestered by reporters at the pub. I let it drop and we never discussed it again.

I followed events in the Evans case as they unfolded over the years and I was relieved when Mr Justice Brabin came to the conclusion that although Evans might have been wrongly convicted of murdering his baby, he probably did kill his wife. Personally, I believe that both men had a hand in the murders. There can be little doubt that Christie was involved and, from the way that Evans behaved at his execution, I think he was too. They say that he was not very intelligent and he was undoubtedly terrified when we walked into his cell, but I just cannot believe that a completely guiltless man would go to the gallows without a last proclamation of innocence. Evans did not utter a single word, not a sound.

Yet I have to admit that it is impossible to be certain. Who knows what Evans expected was going to happen that morning? Did he believe that in the final moments he would be asked if he had anything to say? If he was steeling himself to declare his innocence in a final speech on the trapdoor, he must have realized in the last split second of his life, as he stood hooded, with the rope round his neck, that it was too late ...

6   'You Will Hang by the Neck …'

It is a curious thought that in early Victorian times there were probably very few people who had not seen an execution. Now, a mere hundred years later, there were very few people who had. The official policy had spun completely; having believed it was a most desirable thing for the people to see exactly what happened to a condemned felon, the authorities had now arrived at a position where it was a mysterious official secret.

In the absence of genuine information, the wildest stories were told and believed. Gruesome reports circulated of nightmare scenes in which condemned people had to be dragged screaming and pleading to the trap, where the rope had to be forced round their necks and they were dropped to strangle, moving and twitching for minutes on end. Even the newspapers were years out of date when they reported last walks to execution sheds.

The reality was that the system had been constantly refined and improved to make it as swift and as humane as possible. In addition the chief executioner, Albert Pierrepoint, was the most experienced judicial hangman the world had ever seen. Pierrepoint has never revealed how many people he despatched, but around this time he told me the figure was 688. At nine o'clock in the morning, an execution could be carried out before the local town hall clock had finished chiming the hour.

Nevertheless, so effective was the blanket of secrecy which had been thrown over the whole business that few knew how astonishingly quick it was. In particular, the men who were waiting to die did not know. Regrettably their ignorance added to their fear in many cases.

A screw who had been on death watch duty told me that as the time for the execution drew nearer, the condemned man almost always tried to find out what was going to happen to him. The warders were under orders not to tell him anything.

The screw said the questions were always the same – and so were the answers:

Where is it?

Not far.

The yellow door – what's through there?

Nothing. It's just a storeroom.

Does it take long?

No, it's over very quickly.

Will it hurt?

No, you'll not feel a thing.

The aim was always to calm and soothe during the long, sleepless nights. Over and over again the message: If you have to go, it's better if you go quietly and quickly. It's better for you and it's better for everybody. Go quietly and quickly.

The uncertainty added to the fear of the condemned man yet ironically it made our job – and therefore his death – easier. When it was time, the revelation that he had been living and sleeping a few feet from the gallows could hardly have registered before we had him standing on the drop. He thought he had long minutes to live when he had short seconds. There was no time to fight.

Piotr Maksimowski would probably have faced his death with more courage had he known how quick it was going to be and that he was not going to suffer great agony. We heard that he was obsessed with the idea of wanting to die but he was beside himself with fear at the prospect of hanging.

Maksimowski was a thirty-three-year-old Pole who had been living in the post-war years at a camp at Great Bower Wood near Beaconsfield in Buckinghamshire. He was involved in a tragic love affair with a young woman who lived in nearby Slough. Maksimowski was to claim that they made a suicide pact but unfortunately, while he survived the pact, the woman did not.

The Pole's story was that when he first met thirty-year-old Dilys Campbell she told him that she was a widow. They started going out and got very heavily involved with each other before he was shocked by the news that Dilys was not a widow. Not only was Mr Campbell still very much alive, she was still living with him. Maksimowski said that they both knew the relationship was wrong but they could not stop seeing each other and the affair continued, even though it was making them unhappy and they were ashamed of the way they were behaving. The affair reached its tragic climax in Christmas week. They were together in a pub in Windsor but while the festivities and celebrations went on around them, they had a miserable evening. Eventually they left the pub, Maksimowski intending to go back to the camp alone, but Dilys would not go home and insisted on going back with him in the taxi to Great Bower Wood. Close to midnight they walked in to the wood and there, according to him, she said that rather than going on living like they were doing, it would be better to finish with themselves.

At a quarter to four in the morning, New Year's Eve, there was hammering on the door of the police station at Beaconsfield. The police constable who opened up found Maksimowski standing there, dishevelled and seemingly distraught. He smelt of booze, his shoes were on the wrong feet and his clothes and face were covered in blood. The Pole held out his cut wrists and told the policeman in broken English, 'I did it with a razor. I do same to a girl in the woods. She must be dead – we both wanted to die.'

Police raced off to the woods and in a glade about two hundred yards from the Beaconsfield to Slough Road, they found Dilys Campbell covered with a blanket. Even in the light of their lamps the police could see that there was blood everywhere; Dilys was lying in a pool of it and the grass around was soaked red. She was dead. The police surgeon said she had died slowly.

At the police station Maksimowski was grilled. He stuck to his story that there had been a suicide pact which she had suggested, but the detectives were not buying it. Dilys Campbell's wrists had been cut to the bone whereas it was found that once the blood was wiped off Maksimowski's wrists, the cuts were so superficial that they did not even require stitching. Maksimowski's breathless and dramatic arrival at the police station appeared to suggest a change of heart and a desperate attempt to bring help for the badly injured woman but the medical examination of the body showed that Dilys had been dead for almost four hours before he raised the alarm.

There were scratches on Makzimowski's face and even he admitted that at the end Dilys Campbell had changed her mind and did not want to die. He told detectives, 'We both wanted to die. I cut her with a knife and razor and then she did not want to die. I cut myself. I put a blanket over her.'

The police charged him with murder.

Maksimowski was sent to Warwick Assizes. It was a short trial; although he pleaded not guilty on the grounds of insanity, he did not call any witnesses in his defence, nor did he go into the witness box to give evidence himself. The jury did not take long to reach the guilty verdict and there then occurred what must count as one of the weirdest exchanges ever to take place at such a moment.

In the hushed courtroom the black cap was placed on the head of the judge, Mr Justice Croom-Johnson, and he passed sentence: 'The sentence of the court upon you is that you be taken from this place to a lawful prison and thence to the place of execution and that you be there hanged by the neck until you be dead, and that your body be afterwards buried within the precincts of the prison in which you shall have been confined before your execution. And may the Lord have mercy on your soul.'

Maksimowski, on his feet in the dock, turned and spoke in Polish to the interpreter who had been present throughout the trial. After a moment, the interpreter addressed the judge. 'He has a request to make ... he asks that he should be shot instead of hanged.'

There was a startled silence in the court for several moments, then the judge replied, 'I have no power to deal with the matter. It has passed out of my hands.'

Maksimowski was taken to Birmingham and lodged in the condemned cell at Winson Green Prison to await execution – by hanging. His application to be shot was either ignored or rejected.

Wednesday 29th March was the day set for the execution. I was invited to be the assistant; it was my second execution that month, for the letter from Winson Green arrived only six days after the execution of Timothy Evans. I replied accepting the engagement and at the same time wrote a letter to Pierrepoint to find out if he was to be the number one and suggesting that, if he was, we might meet up for a drink before we went on to the prison.

He wrote back a couple of days later saying that he was to do 'the Birmingham job' but he had an engagement in Liverpool on the Tuesday.

He was having a busy week! Having read the papers, I knew the engagement in Liverpool could only be the hanging of George Kelly, a hoodlum who had gunned down two men during an attempted robbery at a cinema. Pierrepoint would have to be in Liverpool on the Monday to prepare. Kelly would go on the Tuesday morning. Pierrepoint would then travel to Birmingham for the eve of execution routine at Winson Green before the Maksimowski job on Wednesday morning.

In his letter, Albert wrote: 'When you arrive in Birmingham, have a walk round and then make your way to the Police Club in Steelhouse Lane and I will try to get in about 2.00 p.m. If you ask for Inspector Pickard, or Mr Mutch or Mr Thornber – the last two are in the traffic department – they will fix you up until I arrive. You also get a good lunch at the Club – very cheap.'

I did not bother with the lunch but the policemen were as friendly as Albert had predicted they would be, once they knew who I was. We chatted generalities, but I was always reticent in the company of people I did not know and the situation was a little stiff and formal until Pierrepoint arrived at about half past one. The mood of the gathering changed perceptibly; here was the great Pierrepoint hot-foot from one execution and on his way to another. For his part Albert was in a good mood, the centre of attraction. He always felt relaxed, I was to discover, in the company of policemen.

'How did it go with Kelly?' asked one of the people gathered round.

'It was a quick job,' Albert replied, giving the standard answer, but then he added, 'but perhaps we should have done it even quicker.'

What was this? The atmosphere suddenly became expectant, but he would disclose nothing more. Further questions were met with an enigmatic smile and the response, 'You will hear soon enough.'

By this time I had downed a couple of pints and I would have had a couple more, but when one of the policemen asked if I was ready for another, Pierrepoint answered for me. 'Don't forget we've got a job to do,' he said with a meaningful look.

The tone was deceptively mild and he was smiling, but the warning was clear and I declined the offer.

Parting from the policemen with a promise to return tomorrow after the execution, we left, and I could imagine the buzz of speculation that went up as soon as we were out of the doors. I was dying to know what the mysterious comment meant myself and as we reached Albert's car, I could wait no longer.

'Did you have any trouble?' I asked.

'Not really,' he replied, getting inside. 'At least, not at the time. Like I told them, it was a quick job, but the big Liverpool tough-man shit himself!'

I felt the laughter welling up inside me, but one look at Pierrepoint's face was enough to warn me that it would not be well received. I simply said, 'Oh.'

'We didn't realize at the time – we found out when we took him down,' said Pierrepoint, his nose wrinkled in disgust.

'The notorious villain,' I said contemptuously. 'What did you mean when you told the coppers they'll know soon enough … how will they find out?'

'They will,' replied Pierrepoint. 'It'll be halfway round the gaol by now and it won't be long before his friends outside know too … the screws'll make sure of that.'

'This one's not too happy about being hanged,' I said referring to Maksimowski as we drove on to the prison.

'Yes. I read he wanted to be shot,' laughed Pierrepoint.

'I hope this bugger doesn't crap himself,' I said, at last allowing myself to laugh.

'So do I!' said Pierrepoint with feeling.

Winson Green was one of the prisons where Albert got the red-carpet treatment; he was allowed to take his car inside the gaol rather than have to park it nearby and walk through the gate. Strangely it did not happen everywhere, despite the fact that it was obviously a useful convenience when he came to leave after the execution; quite often there were curious people lurking about outside.

We had plenty of time after he got the car parked and, knowing of my keen interest in the history of capital punishment, he asked the warder who was escorting us if we could take a look at the old execution shed. The place was located in the grounds, about thirty or forty yards from the main prison block. Built of brick, it was a tiny place, only about twelve feet square, with double doors at the front.

'It's only used to store garden tools now,' said the warder as he opened one of the doors.

Inside there was little to see. The pit had been filled in and there was nothing on the solid floor to indicate where the trap had been, although clearly it could not have been very big because there was not a great deal of room. The beam had been taken down too. The garden tools were neatly stacked around.

'Nobody comes here much these days,' said the screw. 'Occasionally the guards and prisoners working outside come in to shelter if it's raining heavily.'

I tried to imagine the events which had taken place in this now unremarkable place.

'How long is it since it was used?'

'Near enough twenty years I should think,' he replied, and then pointing to the middle of the floor, he added, 'Stand there.'

I moved to the place he was indicating.

'You're now standing on the very spot where they used to drop them!' he said.

If he was expecting a reaction, he was disappointed. Not a hair on the back of my neck stirred, not a trace of a tingle ran down my spine – but then it's difficult to feel the icy fingers of fear when you're surrounded by spades and rakes and lengths of hosepipe!

'It was a long way for them to come,' I remarked as we left the shed and headed for the main block.

'Aye, it was,' replied the screw. 'They say there was one morning when it was raining cats and dogs, lashing down. The prisoner took one look and told them that he didn't feel like going out in that! They said, 'What are you complaining about – we've got to walk back in it!' It was obviously an oftentold prison yarn, but we had a good laugh.

Inside the main prison building there were matters of more pressing urgency to be attended to, and we found ourselves with a situation on our hands which was certainly no laughing matter. As soon as we got to our quarters Albert was told that the governor wanted to see him immediately. I thought it was a bit unusual but didn't say anything to the tame screw, and in the ten minutes or so that Albert was away the screw gave no indication that anything was afoot.

Pierrepoint arrived back and one look at his face was enough to tell me that something was definitely afoot.

'Anything up?' I asked as casually as I could when we found ourselves alone for a minute.

'Maksimowski has tried to kill himself,' said Pierrepoint quietly.

'Christ!' I breathed.

'Cut his wrists,' continued Pierrepoint.

The suicide attempt had happened three days earlier at eight o'clock in the evening. Maksimowski had apparently just got up from the table – the death watch screws had thought he was stretching his legs – and with no warning he had dashed over to the side of the cell, jumped on the bed or a chair and thrown himself up at the window. He had punched his fists through the wire and glass and then jerked his arms back to slash his wrists on the glass. The warders dragged him off and punched the alarm button. The doctor found that despite all the blood, he had not managed to sever anything vital.

'We're still going ahead?' I asked.

'Yes,' Pierrepoint replied, 'They've patched him up. He's bandaged from his thumb to his elbow.'

'Should that make any difference?'

'No, the governor and the doctor think it should be all-right,' he said. 'Anyway, we're going ahead in the morning.'

Maksimowski had shown, if nothing else, that even a twenty-four-hour, round-the-clock double guard was not enough to stop a determined man trying something desperate. Nevertheless, I thought, the two unfortunate screws would end up with a black mark on their records and I doubted that they would ever do condemned cell duty again, even if they had a mind to. After sixteen days on the duty, on a Saturday evening with the end of their long stint in sight and a prisoner who had caused them no problems, they must have relaxed just that little bit. Needless to say the prison authorities had taken steps to ensure that there was no repeat of the mad episode and an extra guard had been posted in the condemned cell to make sure that Maksimowski did not pre-empt the sentence of the law.

We took a look at the scene of the drama a few minutes later. I was ready for anything when I put my eye to the peephole in the condemned cell door. The place looked crowded with the extra warder in there, but Maksimowski appeared to be as quiet as a mouse. I could see the heavy bandages on one of his arms and beyond where he was sitting at the table, I could see the window – still with the hole which he had punched in the glass.

Albert had taken his look at the prisoner before me, not taking much longer than usual, and then he had wandered off to the execution chamber and was already sorting through the boxes when I followed him. They shut the door on us while they got Maksimowski out of the way.

'His weight's 11 stone 13 – 167 pounds,' said Albert conversationally. 'I'm going to drop him 6 foot 2.'

We worked smoothly and quietly. 'The bandage looked pretty thick,' I said, looking down at him from the ladder where I was adjusting the chains.

'Should be a help,' said Albert. 'Drop it a link ... we won't hurt him with the strap through the bandage.'

During the evening Pierrepoint said nothing about Maksimowski. Not only did he not say anything, I do believe that he did not even think anything about him. To begin with that attitude puzzled me, but I came to realize that it was very simple and not at all inhuman. We had a job to do in the morning and the man had to go. It was not for hangmen to wonder about guilt or innocence or the crime or the sort of man the condemned person was. That sort of thinking created all sorts of problems and anyone who thought like that would, to say the least, not be in the right frame of mind to do the job we had to do – and that was to hang him in the morning. I concentrated on dominoes and the chat and I did not allow myself to think of Maksimowski.

In the morning I confess that I felt less sanguine. We went to the execution chamber and made the final adjustments quite early; it was as trouble-free as the preliminary preparations had been the previous afternoon. It was only during breakfast that I started to get the familiar butterflies, but that was later than normal. I was improving!

On the walk down to the condemned cell I felt sharp and keyed up and, if I am honest, just a touch apprehensive. We did not know what was going to greet us when we went through that door. They said Maksimowski had calmed down after the suicide attempt but nobody could say for sure what was going to happen with someone as frightened and desperate as that.

A minute to go, I looked at the door. There was no sound coming from the other side – a good sign?

Thirty seconds, the governor staring at his watch, Pierrepoint as calmly as you like checking the hood in his breast pocket.

Nine o'clock. Go! The door swung open and I was following Pierrepoint so closely that I couldn't even see past him to Maksimowski. Nothing had happened yet. I looked up at the smashed window. Christ, how had he managed to get up there?

Maksimowski was on his feet, not even looking round. I had hold of his arm, feeling the thick crepe bandages rough under my fingers and bringing the hand up behind him. No resistance. Pierrepoint took it. Two enormous warders stood in close, dwarfing the rest of us; claustrophobically close. I got out the way as Pierrepoint walked off and the warders, taking no chances, jammed up close to Maksimowski. He followed without need of any direction from me.

I got the strap out of my pocket as we walked and held it in my hands ready. The warders were suddenly peeling away and we were on to the trap and moving at a hell of a pace. As Pierrepoint stopped Maksimowski, I bobbed down and got the strap round fast. I was off the trap in a flash and there was a blur and a boom and he had gone!

I knew it had been fast – very, very fast – but I was shattered later when they told us that we had done it in 7½ seconds!

At that moment though, as I went down into the pit, I was just flooded with relief that the worst had not happened. I knew there would be trouble sooner or later and a nut-case like Maksimowski seemed a prime candidate to provide it, but he had, in the end, taken their advice and gone quietly and quickly; my word he had gone quickly. As the doctor listened to Maksimowski's chest, I looked up at the hooded head lolling on one side and I realized that I had helped to hang this man and yet I did not even know what he looked like. All I had seen of him was that brief side-view through the peephole of the condemned cell the previous afternoon.

7 Bungling Bank Robbers

Roman Redel and Zbigniew Gower had to be just about the worst bank robbers of all time. The bungling antics of these two clowns could have been hugely comic … had they not ended with blood running in the streets and the death of a very brave man.

The two Poles, both aged twenty-three, arrived in Britain at the end of the war and settled in Bristol. They were broke, out of work and decided to rob a bank after they rode past it on the top deck of a bus. It looked an easy mark; from their vantage point it was obvious that there was just a single cashier and a rather elderly security man. The bank was a small sub-branch of Lloyds in North View which was manned by Ronald Wall, the cashier, and John Bullock, a retired policeman who was supplementing his pension with the cushy little job as a guard. Redel and Gower planned to hit it during the morning of Monday 13th March 1950.

From the start, everything that could go wrong did go wrong. They got so drunk the night before the robbery that they had to abandon their plans to steal a motorbike, which was to have taken them to the bank and then enabled them to make a quick getaway. They realized that they were quite incapable of riding a bike even if they managed to steal one. They headed to the nearest bus-stop and rode out to their bank raid on a corporation double-decker!

Inside the bank, Redel, brandishing a revolver, soon had Ronald Wall and John Bullock out of the way in an office but Gower, who vaulted over the counter, was starting to panic even as he reached the cash drawer. With half his attention on the office door, he filled his pockets and quickly clambered back over the counter. It was found later that he had grabbed the grand total of £28, and a pile of paying-in slips.

Outside the bank things went from bad to worse. They had no plan of escape and so they jumped on board a bus which happened to be waiting at a bus-stop over the road. They had not locked the bank men in the office, so it was only a few moments before they appeared, and as the bus started to move off, Bullock ran into the middle of the road shouting, 'Stop! Bandits are on your bus!'

All hell broke loose. The driver slammed on his brakes in an emergency stop. John Bullock ran to the platform at the back of the bus but by then Gower and Redel were halfway down the stairs and the security man found himself looking at the business end of the revolver for the second time in as many minutes. 'Stay where you are,' snarled Redel.

Bullock froze and first Gower and then Redel got off the bus and edged past him, the drama now being watched by a mass of disbelieving bystanders. The two Poles turned and fled, but in an instant they were being pursued by a mob which included Bullock, passengers from the bus, people who had been walking in the street, a pick-up truck and a mail van.

A few moments later, the bungling bank robbers were a joke no longer. Redel and Gower were running for their lives but they were no match for one of their pursuers, super-fit judo enthusiast Bob Taylor. He outstripped the hue and cry and ran down Redel, wrapping his arms round the robber. There was a violent struggle and then a loud bang. The thirty-year-old Taylor fell into the gutter, blood pouring from an horrific wound in his head. Redel had shot him.

Redel and Gower escaped the scene but they were picked up by the police within the hour and they were already being questioned by Detective Superintendent Melbourne Phillips at police headquarters when the news came through from the hospital that Bob Taylor had died.

Redel was charged with murder and so too was Gower, even though there was no dispute about the fact that it was Redel's gun, Redel had done the shooting, and at the time Gower was some way ahead. The law was spelt out several times during the trial: if there was a common effort to resist apprehension, they were jointly responsible for Taylor's death. The prosecution claimed that although Redel had fired the shot, Gower was present at all times and was a consenting party to Redel's violence.

In the witness box Gower fought desperately to save himself. There was no plan to resist arrest, there was not even a plan for escaping after the robbery. He did not know the gun was loaded. He did not expect Redel to use it.

Redel was a nightmare in the witness box, and if it was possible to make things worse than they were, he managed to do it. He was exposed as a liar, and when he described the planning of the raid he was almost laughing. His behaviour outraged the judge.

It was an ominously short time before the courtroom was alerted to the news that the jury had reached verdicts. Lawyers hurried back, the judge resumed his position on the bench and the twelve members of the jury filed back in. The foreman delivered their decisions in two brutally short sentences: 'We find Zbigniew Gower guilty of murder with a strong recommendation to mercy. Roman Redel we find guilty of murder.'

The jury's clear desire that Gower should not hang was a pretty accurate reflection of public opinion in this sort of case. There might not be any doubt about the law, but people did not like to see a man swing for a murder he had not actually committed – and Gower had been free and running when Redel used the gun.

Redel was now a dead man. Gower's life was in the hands of the Home Secretary who, acting on the jury's recommendation, could advise the King to grant a reprieve.

While the Pole awaited news of his fate, the preliminary preparations were being made for the execution … preparations for a double hanging. I received a letter from Winchester Prison which informed me the appointed time was nine o'clock on 7th July. The date was a problem because Joyce and I were off to the seaside; we had booked a week in Folkestone from the first to the eighth. I thought about turning the job down but I remembered some advice Pierrepoint had given me very early on: never turn a job down. He did not spell out why, but I was left with the impression that it would count against me if I ever did say no. On the debit side I would lose two days of my holiday; yet on the plus side I would get the chance to visit Winchester, which I had never been to before. I showed Joyce the letter.

'Do you want to go?' she asked.

'I'd like to,' I replied.

'Well if that's it, that's it,' she said, and accepted the situation without complaint.

I replied by return of post, giving them my holiday address in case there was an unexpected turn of events, and I dropped Albert a line thinking we might meet for a drink before the job as usual. I received back a postcard with an amazing reply:

'I think on this occasion you will have to meet me in the place in question because they are making it a hush-hush job. I am being met at the station by the police and taken to the "Hotel" so I shall not be able to have a drink. I think we shall meet on this case so cheerio, hoping to see you – Albert.'

I would have laughed at Pierrepoint's attempt at code had the message not been so dramatic. From his comment, 'I think we shall meet on this case', it was clear which way he thought the pleas for clemency would go. The police escort could only mean that the authorities thought there might be trouble over a decision to hang Gower. In that case – what about me?

There was one snippet of cheery news on the postcard. Pierrepoint had scribbled on the bottom: 'You, Kirk, Allen.'

Harry and Kirky were on the job!

The Saturday before the hanging, Joyce and I headed for the seaside. We had booked into a boarding house at Folkestone and almost as soon as we arrived I joined a library at a shop nearby so that I had plenty of reading material. In the next few days we walked along the sea-front and had ice-creams and ate fish and chips out of newspaper. On days when the weather was fine we sat on the beach, trying to keep out of the bitingly cold wind, and trying to keep the sand out of our packed lunches. By Wednesday I had read seven books and Joyce had made some new friends, a couple who came from Pleasley Vale only a few miles from Woodhouse, who were staying at the same boarding house.

That same day, in London, the final decision had been made in the Home Office and a message was despatched to the authorities in Winchester; the arrangements were to go ahead. There was to be no clemency, both men were to be executed.

Early on Thursday morning I dressed in my suit, brought down specially for the occasion, breakfasted at the boarding house and left for the railway station. Joyce had told her friends and the landlady that I was going to London 'on business'.

In reality I was in London just long enough to change trains at Waterloo Station and I was soon speeding away from the capital. The early part of the journey was uneventful, apart from the pleasure of sitting and watching the unfamiliar towns and countryside flashing by, and, as a railway enthusiast, seeing the completely new types of locomotive running on the Southern Region. As the train neared Winchester the innocent enjoyment of the journey was replaced by grimmer thoughts of the business ahead. Had Pierrepoint needed his police escort? Had there been people intent on stopping the hangman going about his business? Had there been angry scenes at the station? It seemed pretty far-fetched but then so did the idea of a squad of policemen detailed to get him to the gaol in one piece.

I thanked heaven that my photograph had never appeared in the newspapers and that my name was quite unknown to anyone outside a handful of people in official circles. It would have been just too bad if my name had been known, for they made no special arrangements for the assistants, even Harry Kirk. The unflattering truth of the matter was that provided they had a number one the hanging could go ahead. At a pinch they could afford to lose the odd assistant or two – and police cars were no doubt expensive to run!

As the train slowed down on its approach to Winchester Station, I drew a deep breath and collected my bag. I let a few people go ahead of me and then stepped out of the train. The platform looked normal enough, as did the station, and as I walked into the street I found that Winchester looked absolutely normal. It was all a bit of an anti-climax.

I met up with my 'business associates' at the prison and no time was wasted getting down to the preparations. The two condemned men had already been taken out of their cells to a small private yard where they could exercise without being seen by any of the other prisoners. We were shown into a room on the first floor of the prison where it was possible to look through a window down into the yard.

Gower and Redel, each escorted by two prison officers, were walking slowly round the yard. They were kept apart and one man never came much closer than ten yards to the other. Each seemed withdrawn into himself and they scarcely gave each other a glance. Redel was walking with his head down and it was not difficult to imagine what he was thinking about – his hands were round his neck, almost nursing it.

The arrangement was much more convenient than peering through a cell door spyhole and we watched the scene below for several minutes, the men unaware that they were being observed by their executioners. Despite the fact that this was the fifth hanging I was to witness, it was the first time I really had more than a fleeting look at a condemned man, at least alive. They did not, somehow, look much like bank robbers; nor for that matter did they look twenty-three – they seemed older. Redel was the taller of the two, although when we rigged the drop a few minutes later it turned out that Gower was the heavier; he was to get a drop of 7 feet 4 inches compared with Redel's 7 feet 6 inches.

The briefing, from Pierrepoint, came in the execution chamber. Gower, we were told, was next to the drop in the first condemned cell, Redel was further away in the second cell. The positioning seemed a logical way of reducing the danger in those tense but unavoidable few seconds at a double execution when one of the condemned men had to walk on to the scaffold, where he could see the other man waiting with the rope already round his neck. If there was going to be trouble from either of the Poles, it would surely come from Gower who was having to die for the killing that had been done by Redel. As things were planned, he would have no chance to react to the sight of the other man because he would be first into the execution chamber and hooded for a second or two before Redel arrived.

'Kirky, you and Syd go for Redel,' said Pierrepoint. 'Harry will come with me for Gower.'

Execution chambers had an atmosphere about them that I suspect nobody ever really got used to, however many jobs they had done, and despite the fact that we knew the nearby condemned cells were empty, our work was carried out with a minimum of noise or conversation. Pierrepoint and Harry rigged one side of the gallows for Gower while Kirky and I worked on the other side, having been given our instructions about the drop. What few words had to be said were spoken quietly. When Pierrepoint had finished on his side, he checked our work and then told the top screw that he could fetch the governor.

The sandbags were dropped and, satisfied that the scaffold was in perfect working order for the morning, everyone left the chamber and we headed for our quarters, which was when the real fireworks of the day started. Pierrepoint's tantrum came without any warning at all, which made it all the more shocking. The atmosphere as we settled in was relaxed and friendly, there was a hub-hub of banter and conversation. I was talking to Harry, catching up with all the news since we last met in Durham. Kirky was talking to Pierrepoint and the chief warder, and other screws were in and out all the time. I just glanced over casually when another screw walked in with a tray and announced: 'Tea up!'

'What's this?' Pierrepoint's voice cut through the chatter in the room, the tone icy.

There was a deathly hush, I turned round to see what on earth was going on; Pierrepoint was glaring at the table and at the screw who had just come in.

For a second the man seemed shocked at the way he had been spoken to but he quickly found his tongue. 'It's your tea.'

'What is it – bloody grass?' said Pierrepoint sarcastically.

'It's ham and cress salad,' protested the screw.

Pierrepoint looked at it contemptuously and snarled, 'We're not eating that!'

The ham and cress salad did not look the most appetizing meal that I had ever seen – there was a good deal more cress than ham – but I do not think I would have complained. I was stunned by Pierrepoint's nastiness. I had never seen him like this before.

'I said we're not eating that!' repeated Pierrepoint; he was quite obviously livid.

'Well I'm afraid there's nothing else,' said the screw defensively. 'The cook's gone home.'

'Well fetch the bugger back!' demanded Pierrepoint. 'We want summat better'n this – or there'll be no job in the morning!'

'I'll fetch the governor, I'll fetch the governor,' said the screw backing out of the door, leaving the ham and cress salads sitting on the table.

Even when he'd gone, Pierrepoint raved on. 'I'm not eating that muck,' he repeated, and his tone was none too friendly even with us.

No-one else in the room said a word.

'They get money to feed us,' he continued, 'and then they give us this muck.'

The minutes ticked away as we sat waiting for the governor to appear; the tension was almost unbearable – here was the number one threatening not to carry out the job in the morning, indeed threatening to go on strike! Eventually the screw returned. 'The cook's been sent for,' he said and, keeping a watchful eye on Pierrepoint, he gathered up the plates of cress and ham salad and disappeared through the door again.

The new tea, when it eventually arrived, was bacon and eggs – two eggs! There was also a mountain of bread and butter and steaming hot mugs of tea.

'About bloody time an' all,' said Pierrepoint ungraciously, but he had won and he was by that time rapidly cooling off.

For a time the atmosphere in the room remained noticeably strained and I said very little as we ate the tea. It was a completely new side of the number one's personality which had been exposed, a nasty and vicious streak, and I confess that I simply did not understand how such a trivial matter as the tea had unleashed such an outburst. It was much later, when I came to know him better and I had time to talk to other people, that I began to understand what it was all about. It came down to his belief that we were skilled servants of the State, employed to do an important and delicate job, and he was the leader of the team. It infuriated him to think that he and his men could be treated in what he considered a shoddy fashion. In short, he was insulted.

Later in the evening the atmosphere relaxed and we slipped into the familiar eve-of-execution routine; people read newspapers or chatted, there was the inevitable game of dominoes, Kirky was as irrepressible as ever with his fund of funny stories to keep us entertained, and in the end even Pierrepoint came round.

We washed and went to bed soon after ten and I must have only just nodded off when I was woken by an incredible racket. Kirky was snoring and grunting like a hog! With the prison as eerily quiet as they always were on the night before a hanging, the noise sounded loud enough to wake the whole place. I lay for a while trying to shut my ears to the cacophony and get back to sleep but it was impossible; even when he packed up for a minute or two I found myself waiting for him to start up again. I could hear the others moving restlessly and finally Pierrepoint said, 'Are you two awake?'

'You must be joking,' responded Harry Allen.

'Well I'm not listening to this bugger snoring all night,' said Pierrepoint. 'Let's shift him.'

The beds were hospital issue, on wheels, and so we pushed him, still snoring his head off, right down the corridor, as far away from the rest of us as we could move him. He stayed there all night while the rest of us were able, at last, to get some sleep.

We were all up and about the next morning when the squeaking and creaking of the bed wheels heralded Kirky's return. A moment later bed and snorer, still in pyjamas, hove into view. He took one look at the grins and demanded, 'Why did you put me down there?'

'Because you were snoring like a pig!' we chorused in reply, and burst out laughing at Kirky's disbelieving look.

It was the only laughter in the prison that morning, although we did permit ourselves a smile when breakfast arrived; egg, bacon – and a sausage! It was the best breakfast we ever had in gaol.

Down the corridor in the execution chamber, all was in readiness; the final preparations and adjustments had been made even before breakfast. That morning I paid particular attention to the way that Pierrepoint set the safety devices on the lever because he was like greased lightening on a job and they never seemed to slow him down at all. The lever stood in a bracket on the floor and there were two devices to prevent it being pushed accidentally: a pin through the bracket so that the lever couldn't be moved, and a split pin through the end of the main pin so that it couldn't come out accidentally. Pierrepoint first drew the main safety pin as far through the brackets as he could and then put just the tip of the split pin in; it was in, but only just. I could see that all he had to do was give the end of the main pin a sharp tap in the right place, the split pin would drop and the main pin itself would fly clear. The safety devices would not delay him by even half a second.

A few minutes before nine, we walked quietly down through the silent prison and took up our positions. I stood with Kirky outside Redel's cell. Looking down the wing there seemed to be quite a crowd of people; Harry, Pierrepoint and a warder outside the number one condemned cell, and beyond them the governor and under-sheriff and others standing outside a door which led into the execution chamber itself.

At nine o'clock precisely, the governor gave the signal and the warder in front of us pushed the cell door open. Kirky went in and as I followed him I could see out of the corner of my eye that the corridor was emptying rapidly; Pierrepoint and Harry had already gone and further down the landing the party with the governor were moving quickly into the execution chamber.

Inside the cell, a priest was talking to Redel; the two screws on duty got themselves out of our way but stayed close enough to move in if Redel showed any sign of playing up. As we reached the table the priest stopped speaking and Redel rose to his feet; we strapped his arms without any resistance. Kirky started to move out and I gripped Redel's arm to indicate that he should follow. We walked out of the cell through a door, mysteriously and silently opened, which led into the number one condemned cell, now empty apart from another white-faced priest pressing himself back against the wall to be out of the way. Half a dozen paces and we were at the yellow doors and Redel suddenly started; he had caught sight of Gower waiting on the trapdoor, head already hidden from view by the hood and the rope around his neck. He could also see Pierrepoint – and the second noose – waiting for him. For a moment I thought I would have to push him to keep him moving but, after faltering for a couple of steps, he recovered and walked calmly on to the trap where Pierrepoint stopped him on the mark.

As soon as the Pole was still I bent down to strap his legs. In the way that I had practised a thousand times, I whipped the strap round his ankles and icy fingers of fear hit my stomach – the strap was too short! I looked in disbelief at a three-inch gap between the buckle and the end of the strap and as I tried to make them meet the strap slipped out of my fingers and fell on to Redel's shoes! Close to panic I groped for the strap to try again. Above me a strongly accented voice said, 'Do your job properly.'

Even as Redel spoke to me from under his hood, I was easing his legs together, for that was the trouble, and this time I got the strap on and the peg went into the eye. I had not felt any warning tap on the shoulder from Pierrepoint but I still got off the trap as if it was on fire. As I got clear the doors went and Gower and Redel plunged below the level of the floor.

I felt a little shaky as I looked down into the pit where the two men hung. It had been a close call and I learned later that Pierrepoint had spotted that I was in trouble and had deliberately held back for a moment to give me time for the second attempt at strapping the Pole's legs. If he had tapped me

I would not have dared to stay on the trap; Redel would have gone down with his legs free and my career as a hangman would have been over. Most of all I was stunned that a man on the very lip of the grave, a man with less than two seconds to live, had the nerve to speak to one of his executioners and urge him to be more efficient. It had been eerie.

Over a cup of tea in our quarters later, I asked the others if they had picked up the comment. Harry and Kirky, off the trap and standing behind, had not, but Pierrepoint had heard it quite clearly.

'He was a brave man,' I said.

'Aye, he was that,' replied Pierrepoint. 'What happened?'

'I'm not absolutely sure,' I told him. 'His feet were not together but even so the strap seemed very short – I wonder if someone's been helping themselves to a souvenir and chopped a bit off it?'

We had a look at the strap later when we took the bodies down, but we could not tell if a piece had been cut off; if it had, it was not recently. Thanks to Pierrepoint my slip had been minor, the job had gone off well enough and nothing more was said about it. According to Harry and Kirky, Gower had been sullen; they said he had not wanted to go and although he did not actually resist, he had not co-operated either, and they had to pull his arms up to strap him because he would not do anything to help.

It was quiet outside the prison, which was just as well, since the authorities had not laid on a police escort back to the station. Harry went his own way outside the gates and the rest of us travelled into London together, in the guardsvan as it turned out because the train was so full that we could not get a seat anywhere else. Despite the discomfort, we were relaxed and enjoyed the trip, taking turns to have the guard's seat with its projecting window which allowed us to look along the train towards the locomotive. Thankfully Pierrepoint made no protest about the dignity of His Majesty's hangmen and the way they ought to be treated.

At Waterloo I parted from the other two, who were going off to Barney Finnegan's or some other pub to have a few beers. Kirky, fooling around, grabbed hold of me and kissed me goodbye on the cheek! There were people all around and I felt a bloody fool. They walked off leaving me standing there bright red with embarrassment, Kirky's laughter ringing round the station. I caught the Folkestone train and by teatime I was back at the boarding house to enjoy the last few hours of my holiday at the seaside; Joyce and I were returning home to Nottinghamshire in the morning.

With Redel and Gower in their graves, that, so far as the law was concerned, was the end of the matter, but there is one final thing to be added. Some months later it was announced that Bob Taylor had been posthumously awarded the George Cross, the highest award that can be given to a civilian for an act of heroism.

8 The News Gets Out

Pheasant, rabbit and other locally shot game were still appearing regularly on the Dernley dinner table but in the end the poaching had to stop. It was not my official status as a hangman which caused me to think about what we were doing – although the thought did cross my mind that the prison commissioners might not be too pleased if one of their men ended up in the dock in front of the local magistrates – but Lofty was getting up to some dirty tricks which I could not stomach.

The local landowners would no doubt have disagreed, but I had never seen our outings to the woods as a criminal activity and I did not see myself as a thief. The trips were a lark, a bit of adventure and, if my shooting was up to scratch, there were birds and game for the pot at the end of the afternoon's sport. Lofty always adopted a more commercial approach but the man had no respect for anyone or anything. On one occasion he smashed the chain on a gate to get into a particular piece of woodland when we could have gone a bit further and entered without any difficulty. It was typical of him and there were far too many incidents like it. Things came to a head when he took the battery from a tractor which was parked in a field.

'What the hell do you want that for?' I asked him.

He looked at me as if I was simple. 'Because I can sell it, of course!'

That was the end. You might argue about the rights and wrongs of poaching but there was no way that whipping tractor batteries could be called anything but out-and-out stealing and I wanted no part of that.

I cannot say that I missed the trips to the woods. Life as a hangman was providing all the adventure that I could handle. I was seeing the criminals whose notorious deeds were spread all over the pages of the *News of the World*; I was meeting people like Pierrepoint and Kirk and some of the country's top detectives; above all I was travelling all over the country visiting towns and cities in a way that would have been impossible on a pitman's wages. I felt sheer delight watching the countryside flash past as express trains sped away from Nottinghamshire, and there was plenty of flashing countryside as that year progressed; I think I was involved in more executions than anyone on the list apart from Pierrepoint. It was not a sign of special favour, just the luck of the draw. The offers of engagements as assistant executioner went to each man on the list in strict rotation and they stuck to the rotation regardless of whether the job came off or there was a reprieve. It was possible for one man to do several jobs and get several fees, while another fellow's cases were all reprieved and he did nothing. After my slow start, I hit a patch in which almost every job I was offered came off.

As the months went by I grew in confidence; I knew that I was no longer on trial and that, provided there was no disaster, I was on the list for as long as I wanted to be on it. There was even the prospect, admittedly some way off, of becoming a number one. Inevitably the job lost its mystery but it did not lose its fascination – or its threat of danger. We always had plenty of advice about how condemned men were likely to react when it was time, from doctors, governors, screws, but they did not know for sure what was going to happen when they swung that condemned cell door open for us; then it was up to us and we had to deal with whatever we found inside.

Only six days after the hanging of Redel and Gower, I was back in action with Pierrepoint again, to carry out the sentence on a Somerset labourer who had brutally murdered a simple young lass.

The killing was at Bridgwater. The victim was Lily Palmer, a twenty-six-year-old woman who by all accounts should have been safe in a mental hospital long before she was battered to death; she was mentally defective and had been on the waiting list for an institution for three years but no place had been found for her.

The unluckiest night of Lily's brief life started with a casual meeting as she walked along West Street at about eight o'clock. It would be a gross exaggeration to say that she knew Ronald Atwell; she had met the twenty-four-year-old gasworks labourer just once, when he was shown into the seat next to her at a cinema. This night they recognized each other and Atwell invited her to go for a drink. They went into the Horse and Jockey, where a local farmer called Davey saw them talking and drinking together. It was all very quiet and sober.

They stayed in the pub for an hour and a half and Farmer Davey watched them leave shortly after half past nine. It was a chance in a thousand, for Davey was the last witness to see Lily alive and, less than twelve hours later at his farm, he was the first to see her dead. He was walking from the house to his farm buildings when he caught sight of some clothing fluttering in a hedge in the corner of a field. When he went over to investigate, he discovered the girl's battered and bloody body. She was naked apart from her stockings and shoes; some of her clothing was strewn on the ground, the rest ripped to pieces and flung into the hedge. She had been dead for hours.

Atwell, unaware that there was a man whose testimony could send him straight to the gallows, was trying to behave as normal. He went into the gasworks as usual that morning and it was there that he was picked up by detectives just a couple of hours after Lily's body was found.

Atwell went on trial at Wells Assizes in Somerset where his lawyers, up against a watertight prosecution case which included a full confession, mounted the only defence open to them: not guilty because of insanity.

In the witness box, Atwell made a pathetic attempt to shift some of the blame for his violence on to the girl. He claimed that as they strolled through the fields she told him that she had been with another man a few hours earlier. His story was that he did no more than kiss her once or twice and that as she lay there naked, having undressed herself, he started thinking about her being with another man and changed his mind about making love to her. When he called a halt to things, she shouted that he was slimy and swore at him for taking her into the fields for nothing.

In a quiet and controlled voice, Atwell described how he had battered Lily to death. 'I lost my temper and struck her with my fist, either on the mouth or nose. I think I went on hitting her and then put my hands round her throat. The next thing I remember is just kicking her.'

Atwell stopped speaking for a moment and then added, 'I came to my senses and realized what I had done.'

'What had you done?' asked his lawyer.

In a voice which was scarcely audible even in the hushed courtroom, Atwell replied, 'I had killed her.'

The jury took just six minutes to reach the guilty verdict. The judge, Mr Justice Oliver, said it was the most terrible case of murder he could remember. Atwell did not react.

The hanging was fixed for the morning of Thursday 13th July. The governor of Bristol gaol, where Atwell was being held, wrote to me during the week that I was on holiday at Folkestone and I did not find the letter until I arrived home late on the Saturday night, just five days before the execution. As time was short, I sent a telegram accepting the engagement.

Pierrepoint and I were by now a smoothly operating team but each hanging added to my experience; the Atwell execution was also to add to my knowledge of the catering side of the operation!

It was ironical, following the dreadful rumpus about the tea on the Gower and Redel job at Winchester, but we found ourselves talking to Bristol's catering officer. Pierrepoint made a disparaging remark about some of the meals we had been given.

'It's very difficult', said the catering officer, coming to the defence of his colleagues. 'They make us an allowance to feed you – do you know how much it is?'

'No,' we replied.

'They give us eightpence for each of you,' he declared. 'That's for the whole time that you're here!'

'Eightpence?' I repeated, incredulously.

'It's true,' he said. 'That's supposed to cover your evening meal and your breakfast in the morning. I get one shilling and fourpence for the pair of you!'

'It's not much, is it?' I said, watching Pierrepoint out of the corner of my eye. He said nothing.

'We do the best we can,' continued the catering officer, 'but obviously it can't be anything grand on that sort of money.'

'I agree,' I told him. 'Still, we don't eat much … bit of salad or something like that suits me.'

'Well I'm afraid it's not salad tonight,' said the officer, the joke going over his head.

'Don't worry about it,' I replied magnanimously, trying to ignore the evil look that Pierrepoint was shooting at me!

That morning we were in superb form; Atwell went without

giving us any trouble and the execution was over very quickly indeed. I will never forget the look of utter amazement on the face of the under-sheriff as he stood on the other side of the drop to me, gazing down at the body hanging in the pit on the end of the rope. They did not have many executions at Bristol and he certainly was not prepared for the speed at which we had despatched Atwell.

I led the doctor down below for the medical check and when we got back up into the execution chamber the official party was still there, and indeed seemed reluctant to leave. The prison governor looked over to where I stood with Pierrepoint and told us, 'Most extraordinarily efficient work!'

'I second that!' chimed in the under-sheriff, who still looked a little shattered by it all.

The situation was unreal. Apart from the dead murderer hanging below our feet, it could have been a vote of thanks at a meeting of the local council!

'Thank you sir,' Pierrepoint responded. The governor at last turned to the door and the under-sheriff, with a final disbelieving look at the hooded figure in the pit, scurried after him.

The comments were exceptionally pompous, although I have to admit that I took some pride in their praise. It was, after all, the first time that anyone outside the small group of my fellow hangmen had recognized the new skills which I had acquired. Ironically, within a very short time, recognition was the one thing that I would never be short of ever again. Soon, half of Nottinghamshire, most of Mansfield Woodhouse and all of my friends would know about the new skills that I had acquired. The news was about to get out!

At this time there were only three people in Nottinghamshire who knew that I was a hangman. One was Joyce, another was the police inspector who had witnessed my signature on the official documents, and the third was the manager at Sherwood Colliery, Jock Reid. It had been inevitable that I would have to speak to Mr Reid eventually, but I had no idea what his reaction would be to having an assistant executioner on the payroll and I put off going to see him for as long as I could. In the end I was left with no choice when I was offered an engagement at a time when the welders at the pit were working flat out on a scheme to boost productivity. Someone had hit on the deceptively simple idea that more coal could be brought out of the mine if the tubs in which it was brought to the surface could be made slightly bigger. After a few experiments, we found we could weld an extra six inches of metal on to a tub, which then carried a lot more coal. There were eight or nine hundred of the tubs at the pit and it was established that we could convert them at a rate of about thirty-five a week. The job was given top priority and we were given extra money to get us to rush the tubs through. In the middle of it all one of the official brown envelopes arrived one morning at the house.

Even then I tried to get out of going to see Mr Reid and I first tried talking to my direct boss, the engine wright, Bill Dawson. 'I want a couple of days off, Bill,' I told him.

'Bloody 'ell, Syd,' he exclaimed. 'At a time like this … why do you want it off?'

'I'm sorry, I can't tell you,' I replied.

'Are you ill?' he asked.

'No, nothing like that – but I can't tell you.'

He looked at me quizzically, and finally said, 'Well, you better go and see Reid then because he wants these tubs through as quick as possible.'

So there it was. I had no option but to go and see Reid and I was under no illusions that I would get time off without telling him why. I felt apprehensive about speaking to him but I decided to get it over with and I went to work early the next day so that I could see him before I started my shift.

Jock Reid was a Scotsman of middling height, quite plump, with a ruddy complexion. He had reddish-brown hair, swept back, and was always very neatly dressed. He was also a bastard and could be incredibly nasty; when we had been discussing the plans to alter the tubs he had blown his top with the pit blacksmith and one of the welders because they had been negative, in his opinion. He had bawled them out in front of the rest of us and then ordered them out of his office; it had not been a pretty scene to witness. Mr Reid was the manager of the pit and Mr Reid knew it.

'What's the matter, Dernley?' he asked briskly.

'I want a couple of days off next week,' I told him, 'and Bill Dawson said I'd have to see you.'

'Why do you want the time off?' he asked, a bit gruffly.

'I've got to do a little job …' I started to tell him.

'But what about the bloody tubs?' he interjected.

'I think this is a bit more important than tubs,' I said. 'I've got to go to Birmingham to help hang somebody.'

'Fucking hell!' he exclaimed. For a moment he sat there with a look of sheer astonishment on his face and then he asked me, 'Are you sure?'

'Yes, I'm sure,' I laughed.

'What the hell have you taken a job like that for?' he asked.

'Well, I'm not seeking to be notorious,' I explained, 'but I was just interested in the job.'

He sat there looking flabbergasted. 'Does anybody else know about this?'

'Not round here,' I told him, 'and I'd be grateful if you'd keep it quiet because it's under the Official Secrets Act.'

'What days do you want off?' he asked.

'Tuesday and Wednesday. I have to be at the prison in Birmingham the day before the execution, and we do the job on Wednesday morning,' I explained.

He looked thoughtful for a moment and then said, 'What time do you do the job?'

'Nine o'clock in the morning. Why?'

'Can you get back for the afternoon shift? These bloody tubs are important!'

After that I never had any trouble getting time off from the pit and my secret was safe with Reid. No whisper of what I was involved in ever leaked from that quarter.

Unfortunately, people who should have been just as discreet as Mr Reid did not keep their traps shut. It came out, of all things, because the Prison Commissioners had decided they wanted me on the telephone. There had been some consternation over the Atwell job. They had written to me nine days before the execution but because of my holiday they had not got my reply until Monday, just three clear days before the execution. It was uncomfortably close and there had obviously been some discussion about it; had I not been able to accept, they would have been in trouble.

When I went to collect my fee after the hanging, I was buttonholed by the prison steward. 'You aren't on the telephone are you, Mr Dernley?' he asked.

'No,' I replied.

'Why don't you get one installed?' he suggested.

'Well, to begin with, there's a three-year waiting list!' I told him.

'Hmm,' he mused. 'Write to the telephone manager. Say it's important that you are put on the telephone quickly. Tell them why and state that the information is confidential.'

'Should I mention the Prison Commissioners?' I inquired.

'Yes. Tell them the Prison Commissioners wish to have you on the telephone.'

I did as he advised. I wrote to the telephone manager, I explained that I was an assistant executioner and I said that the Prison Commissioners wished me to have a telephone installed. I particularly emphasized the need for secrecy.

The Post Office – with a three-year waiting list – got round to me in four days!

I was at work when the two men arrived at the house. They had a look at the set-up and told Joyce that as it was Coal Board property they would have to get permission from the pit manager to put a pole in. They disappeared off to the colliery; the next day pole and phone were installed and away they went – leaving the bush telegraph going wild. Incredibly, those two workmen had been told that I was a hangman! When they went to the pit they told the manager's clerk Jimmy Lyons, Jimmy Lyons told somebody else … It was like a stone hitting a pool; the ripples spread and spread.

For several days I had no hint of what was going on. I was working afternoons and nights; no-one said anything to me at the pit and I was not going down to the village. So it was that on Saturday night, a mild summer's evening, I strolled down to The Bull, blissfully unaware of the fact that I had been the main topic of conversation in the pub, and in a lot of other places, for most of the week.

I noticed nothing strange as I walked to the bar and ordered a pint, although when I thought about it later, I realized I must have been half asleep not to sense the atmosphere. I picked my way over to the table where my pals were sitting: Billy Ball, Albert Fisher and Wilf Derby. We met up every Saturday night to play dominoes and sometimes in the week when we could make it. Bill ran a butcher's shop for the Co-op; Albert had his own painting business and employed about fifteen men; Wilf Derby was the manager of a firm of agricultural engineers.

'Evening,' I nodded as I reached the table, where a place had been reserved for me.

'Evening Syd,' they replied with friendly smiles.

We chatted for a few minutes and then, straight out of the blue, Wilf looked at me with a grin and said, 'Well Syd, who are you going to hang next week?'

My heart stopped, I could not believe my ears! I said nothing for a second and then blustered, 'What the hell are you talking about?'

'You know what we're talking about,' retorted Wilf. 'We've heard all about it!'

Indeed they had heard all about it. In fact, the whole bloody pub, everyone at the pit and half the town had heard about it, thanks to the big-mouthed devils from the telephone office.

It was a strange night. I noticed that people all over the room were staring at me when they did not think I was looking. When I went to the bar, conversations died as I walked past people and started up again when I had gone. My friends showed no sign of disapproval; quite the reverse. Billy had a look that was close to adulation on his face when I explained how I had applied for the job and been interviewed and appointed, while Wilf exclaimed, 'Good for you, lad!'

They were bursting to know all about it, but that night they kept their questions to a minimum in the crowded bar. Later I did speak to them more openly, particularly Billy Ball, who was married to my second cousin, but I took my cue from Pierrepoint and talked only in the most general terms and never about specific cases. They wanted to know what happened at an execution, what it was like in prison, did I know Pierrepoint and what was he like? Sometimes when I answered their questions they did not believe me. I remember the look on Billy's face when I explained that it was all over in a few seconds. 'That's impossible!' he gasped. 'It can't be done that quickly.'

Other people whom I hardly knew suddenly became friendly and tried to pump me for information, especially when there was a bad case which grabbed the headlines. They would offer to buy me a drink, which I accepted, and then would come the questions, quite often fuelled by the most lurid imaginations.

'How did the job go?'

'Fine, no problems.'

'Did he scream?'

'No, he didn't.'

'Did he struggle?'

'No, the job went off quickly.'

Stock answer: the job went off quickly. They were not the sort of people whom you would tell that the execution had been carried out expeditiously. More questions would follow, to be stonewalled, sometimes gently, sometimes not so gently. They no doubt thought I was uncommunicative, perhaps even surly; the truth was that I was dying to talk to someone openly about it but I just dare not.

It was astonishing how quickly and how far the news travelled. In the next few weeks, people stared at me in the street and even when I went into a pub in Mansfield there was somebody in there who had heard; the word went round and soon there were people craning to get a look at me, or more accurately craning to get a look at the hangman. I felt quite the celebrity.

I particularly enjoyed a very detailed report of one conversation between a mate of mine at the pit and Les Rowe, the senior welder and no friend of mine.

'Have you heard about Syd Dernley?'

'What about him?'

'He's a hangman!'

'Him!' laughed Rowe. 'He couldn't hang wallpaper!'

'It's true I tell you!'

'Some people believe anything,' was Rowe's derisive response.

'He's had a lot of odd days off, hasn't he?'

'Yes.'

'And he had a couple of days off just after he'd got back from holiday.'

'That's right.'

'That's because they were hanging some bloke in Bristol.'

'Christ!' said Rowe, and by all accounts he looked quite shocked.

After a while the regulars at The Bull got used to having a hangman in their midst and made very little of it apart from occasions when I had not been down for a few days and there had been an execution somewhere in the country. Quite often I had not been involved but there would be a sudden hush descend on the place when I walked in. I have bought pints in a crowded bar where you could have heard a pin drop!

They could not resist joking about it, of course. 'Where's Wilf tonight?'

'He's playing dominoes with the hangman.'

'Hope he doesn't ask whose drop it is!'

The landlord had a favourite: 'Here's Syd. Make space you lot, no hanging round the bar!'

9 'I Want to Hang'

One July morning in 1950, an old cargo ship made her way slowly up the River Tees on the north-eastern coast of England. The best days of the SS *Absalon* had long since passed but she had been sturdily built in the West Hartlepool yard of Gray and Company in 1898, she had survived two world wars and she was still afloat despite her advancing years. I doubt that anyone took very much notice of the arrival of this tired old steamer and yet this was the inauspicious start of one of the strangest cases I was ever involved with. I never came àcross a killer who came closer to getting clear away. I certainly never met another man who chose to hang, rather than try to save his neck and serve a prison sentence.

The 2,000-ton ship gently edged alongside the wharf at Billingham Reach and as the mooring ropes were made fast, the master rang down that he was finished with the engines. The *Absalon* was tied to the land for the three days that it would take for her cargo of sugar to be unloaded and the stage was set for the drama which was to ensue.

Below deck, one of those who heard the bridge telegraph ring out was the third engineer, Patrick Turnage. Thirty-one-years-old, Turnage had been born in India, although he now had his home in South Africa, in Congella near Durban.

The next few days were uneventful; the *Absalon*'s cargo was taken off and the captain decided that he would put to sea again late on Sunday 30th July. It meant the chance of a Saturday night ashore for some members of the crew and among the lucky ones was Patrick Turnage. Determined to waste no time, he took a bus into town early in the evening and with a sailor's unerring nose for such matters, he homed in on the bus conductor as a likely lad with useful local knowledge. They chatted for a while and Turnage asked where he could find a

116

woman. The obliging busman pointed him in the direction of the Victoria Hotel in Joseph Street.

A little earlier in the evening an old lady, more than twice Turnage's age, had also been getting ready for her night out. Julia Beesley was seventy-eight. She had been a widow for a quarter of a century and now lived with her son at a house in Northbourne Road at Stockton. For the most part Julia's life revolved around the local old people's club of which she was a popular member, but at the weekend she got dolled up and went into town where she normally got drunk. The truth of the matter was that Julia was an old prostitute who, incredible as it sounds, was still plying her trade at the age of seventy-eight!

It will perhaps come as no surprise that in the early part of the evening Julia had little luck, but over the years, as her charms faded, she must have become well used to the rebuffs of sober citizens and undeterred she drank here, drank there and pressed on. She had visited various pubs in the town centre when, quite late in the evening, she arrived at the Victoria Hotel, a little the worse for wear.

Behind the bar, the holiday relief manager, Tom Davies, noticed the tipsy old woman. She was still drinking, despite the fact that she was none too steady on her feet, and she kept going up to men in the bar and talking to them. Tom kept an eye on her in case the pestering of his customers got out of hand, but towards closing time in the crowded bar he lost sight of her and, breathing a sigh of relief, assumed that she had left the hotel.

What he didn't realize was that Julia, still out of luck, had moved on only as far as the pub's buffet bar where her prospects suddenly improved. There she came across Patrick Turnage who, despite the conductor's advice, had also enjoyed no luck; he had been knocking back the pints all night and was now well drunk. The old pro moved in and began talking to the seaman, and this time she was not rebuffed. A short time later they rolled out of the pub together, and after some supper Turnage suggested they go back to his ship for drinks. At midnight he flagged down a taxi and the pair of them rode back to the wharf where the *Absalon* was moored.

'Is the taxi waiting for me?' asked Julia as she got out of the car.

'No, I'll get him to come back for you later,' said Turnage.

As the old woman walked away, Turnage turned to pay the

fare and said under his breath to the driver, 'She'll be staying all night.'

The taxi driver grinned and left.

Julia Beesley was, though, neither as drunk nor as daft as the seaman seemed to think. Julia never spent the night with her clients and seemingly she was not about to start now. On board the *Absalon* the watchman saw the taxi pull away and looked on as Turnage and the woman approached the ship. They got as far as the wharf edge and then there seemed to be some sort of trouble. There were raised voices. Julia was refusing to go on board the ship and then she abruptly turned on her heel and walked away. Turnage watched her disappear; for several minutes he stood on the quay but then he went after her.

It was an hour before he returned alone and climbed down on to the ship. 'Did you see her?' asked the watchman.

'No, I couldn't find her,' replied Turnage, who carried on walking towards his cabin, without stopping to talk further. In the poor light, the watchman did not notice that Turnage was carrying a woman's handbag.

At eleven o'clock the next morning, Julia's son Robert, thoroughly alarmed that she still had not returned home, alerted the police, and the missing woman's description was circulated to the officers patrolling the town.

The wharf was a hive of activity as the SS *Absalon* prepared to shake herself free of the land once more. The master was anxious to be on his way and said he would be sailing on the tide in the early evening. He was not the only one on board keen to get away; third engineer Patrick Turnage must have found it difficult to tear his eyes away from the clock.

The hands had moved round to two and work on the *Absalon* was all but complete when chargehand navvy John Walker mounted his bike and cycled off home for his Sunday dinner. John had almost reached the main road when something caught his eye in the ditch at the side of the lane. Dozens of people had been up and down to the wharf that morning but the curious navvy got off his bike and walked to take a closer look. Scrambling down into the ditch, he pulled aside a heap of grass and found to his horror that he was looking at the body of an old woman. John Walker had found the missing Julia Beesley.

The first policeman arrived on the scene within minutes of the alarm being raised, took one look, and immediately called for help. The lane was sealed off and the area was soon crawling with detectives. It looked a funny one; clearly there was no reason why the old woman should be near the wharf, and beyond a shadow of doubt there had been an attempt to hide the body – it had been covered with grass – but strangely there did not seem to be a mark on it. How had she died?

Julia's body was left where it was until Detective Chief Inspector John Rowell arrived a little later to take charge of the investigation. He had a look and a short time later gave the order for the corpse to be removed to the morgue. Home Office pathologist Dr David Price had been alerted and he was already on his way from Leeds.

How swiftly can success become disaster! At lunchtime Turnage must have started to relax. People had been up and down the lane to the wharf all morning and the old woman had not been found; in a few short hours the *Absalon* would be casting off, sailing out of the Tees, and he no doubt already had plans to leave the ship at the first suitable point and disappear, never to be heard of again. He must have felt that he was home and dry ... but now how slowly must the hands of the clock have moved as he waited for the tide, and the detectives came ever closer.

The policemen beat the tide. A detective constable came for Turnage at half past five. Turnage crumbled. He made no attempt to deny that he had been with the woman. He produced Julia's handbag and gave it to the detective.

News of Turnage's arrest was immediately despatched to Detective Chief Inspector Rowell who was now at the morgue, but for the moment he was more interested in what Dr Price had to say. The pathologist went to work early in the evening and soon had the answers the detective needed: Julia Beesley had been dead since the early hours of the morning and, in his opinion, death had been due to asphyxia as the result of the application of pressure to the neck. Mrs Beesley had been strangled.

But why were there no marks, asked the policeman. Dr Price explained that it was possible the pressure on the neck could have been produced merely by tightening and twisting the clothing round her neck. It had not taken much to kill her.

At Billingham police station, Turnage was getting a good grilling, but over and over again he denied that he had deliberately killed Julia. He claimed that they had quarrelled when she made sexual suggestions to him. 'I told her not to be silly as she was old enough to be my mother. She called me all the names in the dictionary. I just gave her a push and she fell into the ditch.'

Turnage said he felt sorry as soon as he had done it and scrambled down to help her out. 'I went to pick her up and discovered that she was limp. I looked for some water as I thought she'd just fainted. I went back to the watchman's hut but there was nobody there. I tried to lift her again but she was still limp.'

As a policeman took notes, Turnage claimed that he had then panicked. 'I didn't know what to do. I was so worried and frightened I could not think straight. I went back to the ship and was too frightened to say anything to anybody about what had happened.'

Turnage was lying, of course; his interrogators knew it and the investigation over the next few days was to prove it. His claim that the old prostitute had propositioned him did not square with his whispered comment to the taxi driver that she would be staying, nor did it square with his conversation with the busman, when he had made it clear that he was after a woman. His explanation of events also begged the question: If he was not considering going to bed with Julia because she was old enough to be his mother, why was he taking her back to his ship?

Most incriminating of all, he had said that he just gave her a good push ... But Julia had not died of a fall; the pathologist said she had been strangled.

Despite the lies, the detectives who considered the situation, particularly late that first night, were not sure that they could make a murder charge stick. A seventy-eight-year-old prostitute who was still on the game was scarcely going to elicit great sympathy from a jury and if all it took to do her in was to grab the clothing round her neck and twist ... In short, it looked touch and go, and the smart money went on Turnage escaping on a manslaughter charge, for which he could not be hanged.

Without wishing to appear gratuitously callous, the case thus far had been a fairly run-of-the-mill crime which had been solved quickly; it attracted little interest from the national newspapers and so it remained for the next few weeks. Turnage regularly appeared before the magistrates whilst the case against him was being prepared, and a month later he was committed for trial to Durham Assizes. The case was to go into court on Thursday 28th October and it was just forty-eight hours before it started that matters began developing rapidly in a completely unforeseen way. The first indication of something out of the ordinary came when Detective Chief Inspector Rowell received a message from Durham Prison where Turnage was being held. The prisoner was asking to see him!

The detective made the short trip to Durham late in the afternoon and arrived at the prison just after five o'clock. He was shown into a room in the hospital wing and Turnage was brought from his cell. Face to face with the man who was trying to send him to the gallows, Turnage said, 'I want to plead guilty to the charge.'

Even the senior detective, who no doubt thought he had seen the lot before, was taken aback, and with good reason – nobody pleaded guilty to a capital murder charge! It did not matter how bad the crime, it did not matter how weak the defence was, nobody went into the dock and pleaded guilty. Even the Christies of the world, with bodies all over the place, pleaded not guilty! Such a plea could mean only one thing ...

'You do realize the consequences of what you're saying?' the detective warned Turnage.

'Yes I do,' replied the man, who was now positively running at the gallows.

'I would advise you to speak to your legal representative,' warned Rowell.

Turnage was having none of it. 'My mind is made up and I want to speak the truth. I knew what I was doing and I knew she was dead when I left her. I did not expect her to be found and I was sailing the next day.'

Turnage's solicitor was hurriedly summoned to the gaol, and later that evening there was another meeting between Turnage and Rowell, with the lawyer present, at which the seaman again insisted that he was pleading guilty.

The situation caused consternation – the man was putting the noose round his own neck. There could be no defence now; there was no way that skilful argument could perhaps sway the jury and save him from the drop – there would be no jury. Turnage had decided to be hanged. There could be no other outcome to this amazing situation.

Rowell wanted to take a statement, but after discussing the position with Scott, the solicitor, he agreed to hold off for a few hours so that Herbert Shepherd KC, who had been briefed to lead for the defence, could be alerted to the sensational situation which was developing in his case. Shepherd went to the gaol on Wednesday afternoon, the eve of the trial, and at their meeting Turnage was as determined as he had been the previous day that he was going to admit to the crime and plead guilty. Shepherd could do no more than acquiesce to the prisoner's wishes and a short time later the police got their statement. In the confession Turnage described in detail how he had strangled Julia Beesley and he made it clear that the killing had been premeditated.

The next morning Turnage was brought up into the dock at Durham Assizes and the charge was read to him. When asked how he pleaded, he answered, 'Guilty.'

The judge, Mr Justice Hallett, had been forewarned of the plea but because of the gravity of the situation made doubly sure. Addressing counsel for both prosecution and defence he said, 'When such a plea is tendered by a prisoner in answer to such a charge, it is the clear duty of the court, before accepting the plea, to assure itself that it represents the advised and settled determination of the prisoner.'

Turning to the prosecution counsel, the judge continued, 'Accordingly, Mr Hinchcliffe, I think it would be desirable that you should call the detective chief inspector to give evidence in accordance with the additional evidence I have received.'

Detective Chief Inspector Rowell was then called into the court to relate what had happened in the past forty-eight hours. It was the only evidence taken.

The judge then addressed Turnage: 'Having regard to the evidence I have heard, it is quite clear that the plea which you have tendered to the court has been tendered by you after careful consideration and with the benefit of advice by your solicitor and counsel. Accordingly it remains only for me to pass the sentence prescribed by law.'

Mr Justice Hallett paused while the square of black material was placed on his head and he then sentenced Turnage to death. The proceedings from start to finish had taken only seven minutes.

There being no appeal, setting the date for the execution was a simple matter for the authorities. According to the rules governing these things, there had to be three clear Sundays, and therefore I was engaged for Tuesday 14th November. When I contacted Pierrepoint I found out that he had already accepted an engagement somewhere else and the number one's job had gone to Steve Wade – scarcely the best of news.

In fact, on this occasion Wade did not seem as nervy as he had been at our first meeting, but I still did not feel comfortable with him and I did not think he was as good an executioner as Pierrepoint, a feeling which was not helped when we came to rig the gallows. I noticed with surprise that he intended to drop Turnage 7 feet. The seaman was 5 feet 8 inches tall and weighed just under 11½ stones. He was young and strong but I knew from the table of drops, which I had memorized, that on that weight he should be getting something around 6 feet 3 – 9 inches less. Wade did not explain his reasoning to me and, of course, I did not question his decision. He was the number one, it was up to him.

Back in the hospital wing we said very little to each other and I found myself thinking that it was going to be a long, long night. Fortunately, when the warder who was to stay with us arrived, he turned out to be a very talkative and amusing bloke who single-handedly saved the situation and averted what, as like as not, would have been an almost silent evening. Even so it was a relief after tea when Wade was summoned to the governor's office and his staid and oppressive presence was removed for a while. In the half an hour or so that he was away, I got the lowdown on the extraordinary situation which prevailed in the condemned cell.

'How is he?' I asked, nodding in the direction of the execution suite.

'Cheerful,' replied the screw with a grin. 'Cheerful as could be!'

'Cheerful!' I echoed in astonishment.

'Not a word of a lie,' said the screw. 'He's quite happy – this one wants to go!'

'Has he gone crackers?' I asked.

'No. The lads in the condemned cell with him say he's perfectly OK. Just wants to get it over with.'

'Incredible,' I said; it all sounded too unbelievable for words.

'You know he pleaded guilty at the trial?' asked the screw.

'Yes, I read that.'

'Apparently he killed the old tart because she asked him for a pound,' the screw continued.

'Christ!'

'Some of the coppers said he needn't have been hanged at all.'

I listened open-mouthed.

'Some of our lads were talking to a couple of detectives on the case. They were amazed when he decided to plead guilty to murder. They thought he could have escaped the gallows if he had pleaded manslaughter.'

'Why on earth didn't he plead manslaughter then?' I asked.

'He told the police he'd prefer the drop to fifteen years in stir,' replied the screw.

'That's incredible!' I responded.

The screw agreed it was incredible, everyone agreed it was incredible, but the fact remained that in the execution chamber a heavy sandbag was hanging on the end of a rope in the yawning pit and, so far as Patrick Turnage was concerned, the lights were burning through the night in the condemned cell for the last time.

'I wouldn't give a bugger what the gaol was like or where it was,' I said, 'I know what I'd choose!'

'Me too!' agreed the screw.

When Wade returned he confirmed that Turnage was expected to go quietly in the morning. He also said that the seaman had asked if one of the condemned cell guards could be with him at the execution, a request which came as no surprise to our tame screw who said that Turnage had got on well with him over the past few weeks. Wade said the condemned man's request had been agreed to.

The relationship between a man under sentence of death and his gaolers was always a difficult one and it quite often developed in very strange ways. Surprisingly, screws I talked to over the years said it was not uncommon for a kind of friendship to develop and for the condemned cell duty men to become sympathetic with their prisoner in his plight. They were together for weeks on end in that small cell in an atmosphere of unremitting tension and strain. They talked if he wanted to talk, they played cards if he wanted to play cards, they were silent if he wanted silence. They had to calm him down and keep him under control when the strain became almost too much to bear. They wondered almost as much as he if there would be a reprieve … and they had to cope with the collapse of hope when there was not.

The system recognized what could happen and indeed used it to keep the man under control. The authorities were also alive to the strain that it could put on their men, and the warders who had been on condemned cell duty were not expected to be involved in the execution. The last two were pulled out a few hours before the time and two strangers were brought in, unless the prisoner requested otherwise.

In my experience it was fairly rare for such a request to be made, although clearly it was not unheard of because the authorities had laid down a rule about it and the request was always granted, as it was in this case. No-one ever explained to me why a condemned man should care who was with him as he walked to the gallows. I guessed that it was perhaps as simple as wanting a friendly face there to help him keep up his courage in the final few moments. The authorities of course would agree to anything that calmed the man down and ensured that he did not kick up a fuss in those delicate and dangerous seconds when we went to work.

They need not have worried about Patrick Turnage. The next morning he got his wish. He escaped his fifteen years in stir, and went as cheerfully to his grave as they said he would. When they swung the condemned cell door open for us, the seaman turned to watch us enter. For just a moment there was a flicker of fear, and then his face changed and I swear he smiled at us! It was spine-chilling! Automatically, I carried on walking towards him but with my face set; I could no more have returned his smile at that moment than I could have walked through the solid brick walls of the condemned cell!

When we had secured his arms with the strap, one of the warders, who was obviously the friend he had asked to be with him, gently touched his shoulder and nodded after Wade who was leading the way into the execution chamber. Shoulder to shoulder they walked out of the condemned cell, through the yellow doors and on to the trapdoors of the gallows.

Turnage's manner and self-control was one of the most remarkable things I ever saw on an execution morning. How shocked the hanging public would have been if they had known how little he feared the gallows. He was guilty of a bizarre and disgusting crime and perhaps in the end it was the shame which weighed so heavily on his conscience that made him decide not to fight for his life. Had he successfully pleaded manslaughter and his fears of a fifteen-year prison sentence been proved correct, he would still have been only forty-six years old when he was released from prison.

As the express train sped away from Durham later that morning, I reflected on the strange eddies of fate which could leave a sailor rotting in an unmarked prison grave in the north-east of England, so far away from the sunny climes of home. The SS *Absalon* had long since steamed her weary way out of the Tees, leaving the whole tragic mess behind her. I wondered if sailors who suffered violent deaths returned to haunt their ships. It would have been the height of irony if Turnage, the man who could not bear the thought of fifteen years in gaol, returned to the *Absalon*, for within a few short months her days of steaming the oceans of the world were over for ever, her human crewmen gone. She was turned into a moored hulk, a rotting shell far worse than even the most awful of His Majesty's prisons.

10   A Rotten Job

As a long-time student of the history of the craft, I knew that one of the most horrific botch-ups in the annals of British hanging occurred at Norwich Castle in November 1885. Down the centuries there had been awful scenes at executions when things went wrong, primarily because of their technique. The condemned criminal was not dropped far enough to break his neck, quite often not even far enough to render him unconscious, and he slowly strangled to death on the end of the rope. The only thing that could be done to help was for the hangmen to swing on the legs of the poor wretch to bring his suffering to a slightly quicker end. It was as a result of horrendous scenes like this that a Victorian executioner called William Marwood experimented with, and then introduced, the long-drop method which broke the neck and brought instantaneous death. Without any shadow of doubt the new system despatched the condemned person more humanely, but ironically the technique brought with it the possibility of a new horror which, for the people present at an execution, was far worse than anything which could have been produced by the old method.

In 1885 James Berry was engaged to carry out the hanging of a man called Robert Goodale who had been sentenced to death for the murder of his wife. Goodale was an enormously fat man who even at the time he was due to die, when he had presumably lost quite a lot of weight, still turned the scales at over fifteen stones. I do not believe for a moment that we would have risked hanging such an obese man because of the danger of things going wrong; he would just have been reprieved. Berry made special plans; at the time he was still working on what was essentially Marwood's table of drops, and according to that Goodale ought to be given a fall of 7 feet 8 inches. Berry was uneasy about such a long drop and decided to reduce it by almost 2 feet; he would give Goodale only 5 feet 9 inches.

Meanwhile, if Berry was anxious about the hanging, some of the prison staff were in a state verging on panic. The week before the execution, on the Thursday, the governor of the prison had the gallows tested. They worked satisfactorily but he was still not happy, and had them tested again two days later, on the Saturday. Berry makes it clear that the man was in a bit of a state by the time the morning of the execution dawned. In his memoirs, Berry left a graphic description of what happened.

> The whole of the arrangements were carried out in the usual manner and when I pulled the lever the drop fell properly and the prisoner dropped out of sight. We were horrified, however, to see that the rope jerked upwards and for an instant I thought the noose had slipped from the culprit's head or that the rope had broken. But it was worse than that for the jerk had severed the head entirely from the body and both had fallen into the bottom of the pit. Of course death was instantaneous so that the poor fellow had not suffered in any way; but it was terrible to think that such a revolting thing should have occurred. We were all unnerved and shocked. The Governor, whose efforts to prevent any accident had kept his nerves at full strain, fairly broke down and wept.'

Berry himself was badly shaken by the Goodale mess but he was made of stern stuff; drawing on his experience he revised the table of drops, and he continued as the country's main executioner for several more years.

I mention this gruesome piece of hanging history because my next job was to take me to Norwich, my first visit to the city, and although the execution was to be at the new prison, rather than at the castle where the Goodale hanging had taken place, I was very conscious of the story. I thought even more about it after what happened to us. Who says lightning does not strike in the same place twice?

However, I race ahead of myself. Let me first sketch in the background and circumstances which led up to one of the most unfortunate hangings I was ever involved with, indeed one of the most unfortunate hangings that anyone was involved with in this century.

The story begins on a Friday evening in August 1950 in the small east coast port of Yarmouth. At a variety of pubs in the

Syd Dernley with Joyce Harston at the time of their engagement.
They married in October 1943.

Hangmen and friends after an execution at Shrewsbury.
Left to right: a reporter, Albert Pierrepoint, a pub landlord and
Syd Dernley.

Memorandum of Conditions to which any Person acting as Assistant Executioner is required to conform.

(An Assistant Executioner will not be employed by the Governor without the concurrence of the High Sheriff.)

1. An Assistant Executioner is engaged, with the concurrence of the High Sheriff, by the Governor of the prison at which the execution is to take place, and is required to conform with any instructions he may receive from or on behalf of the High Sheriff in connection with any execution for which he may be engaged.

2. A list of persons competent for the office of Assistant Executioner is in the possession of High Sheriffs and Governors : it is therefore unnecessary for any person to make application for employment in connection with an execution, and such application will be regarded as objectionable conduct and may lead to the removal of the applicant's name from the list.

3. Any person engaged as an Assistant Executioner will report himself at the prison at which an execution for which he has been engaged is to take place not later than 4 o'clock on the afternoon preceding the day of execution.

4. He is required to remain in the prison from the time of his arrival until the completion of the execution and until permission is given him to leave.

5. During the time he remains in the prison he will be provided with lodging and maintenance on an approved scale.

6. He should avoid attracting public attention in going to or from the prison ; he should clearly understand that his conduct and general behaviour must be respectable and discreet, not only at the place and time of execution, but before and subsequently ; in particular he must not give to any person particulars on the subject of his duty for publication.

7. His remuneration will be £1 11s. 6d. for the performance of the duty required of him, to which will be added £1 11s. 6d. if his conduct and behaviour have been satisfactory. The latter part of the fee will not be payable until a fortnight after the execution has taken place.

8. Record will be kept of his conduct and efficiency on each occasion of his being employed, and this record will be at the disposal of any Governor who may have to engage an assistant executioner.

9. The name of any person who does not give satisfaction, or whose conduct is in any way objectionable, so as to cast discredit on himself, either in connection with the duties or otherwise, will be removed from the list.

10. The apparatus approved for use at executions will be provided at the prison. No part of it may be removed from the prison, and no apparatus other than approved apparatus must be used in connection with any execution.

11. The Assistant Executioner will give such information, or make such record of the occurrences as the Governor of the prison may require.

(C31191) 100 6/50

The rules – two copies were sent with every offer of an engagement; one copy had to be signed and returned.

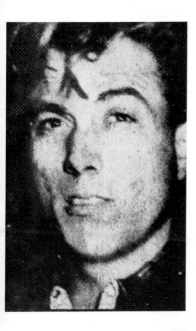

Edward Devlin, though a hard man who gave an arrogant performance in court, crumbled in the condemned cell.

Alfred Burns believed he would be freed and was planning his revenge on the prosecution witnesses. On 27th February 1952 he was hanged in Liverpool.

To S. DERNLEY Esq

"BEFORE I SUM UP THIS IS JUST TO DEMONSTRATE BEFORE THE COURT <u>WHY</u> I AM KNOWN AS THE HANGING JUDGE"

Merry Christmas! Hangmen had their fans one businessman sent Sy a specially commissioned card every year.

The gallows – Syd made a miniature model. It is an exact replica of the real thing on a scale of one inch to the foot.

The Hull murderer James Inglis arriving at court handcuffed to a detective. Inglis was hanged at Manchester on 8th May 1951.

H. M. PRISON,
Pentonville,
London, N.7.
22nd February, 1950.

Mr. S. Dernley,
10, Sherwood Rise,
Mansfield Woodhouse,
Mansfield,
Notts.

Dear Sir,

141 Timothy John EVANS.
Offence: Murder. Sentence: Death.

The appeal of the above named man has been dismissed and the High Sheriff of the County of London has fixed Thursday, the 9th March, at 9 a.m. for the execution.

I am forwarding a Railway Warrant for your journey and I shall be glad if you will report to the prison not later than 4 p.m. on Wednesday, the 8th March. Accommodation will be provided for you.

Will you please acknowledge receipt of the Railway Warrant and confirm that you can accept this engagement. A stamped addressed envelope is enclosed for your reply.

Yours faithfully,

Governor.

a bone repoint.

Drop. 8'0"

15 secs.

Evans arriving back in London with detectives (*insert*). He did not know that the police had found the bodies of his wife and child, who had both been strangled.

The official letter detailing the arrangements for the execution of Timothy Evans, later granted a posthumous pardon. Immediately after the hanging, Syd scribbled brief notes on the letter – the name of the number one, the drop and the time.

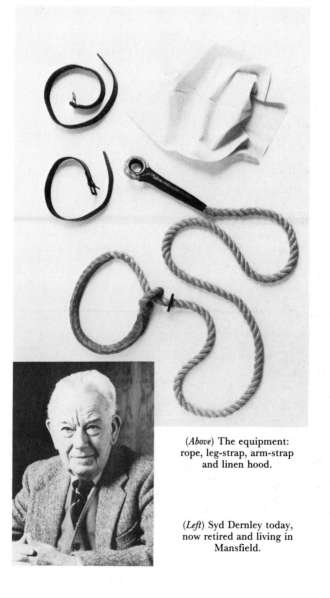

(*Above*) The equipment:
rope, leg-strap, arm-strap
and linen hood.

(*Left*) Syd Dernley today,
now retired and living in
Mansfield.

For many years, Syd had the only privately owned gallows in the country erected in his cellar. Here he shows a student friend the ropes.

Hanging on the air. Syd Dernley and David Newman began their collaboration on *The Hangman's Tale* after a programme about capital punishment on Radio Trent. In the background, presenter Gary Burton engineers the discussion.

town that night, a man called Norman Goldthorpe was swilling back the beer; he was on a bender. Goldthorpe was a small man, only half an inch over five feet tall, but he could be a nasty piece of work and tonight the little man had a towering rage building up inside him. He had been left in the lurch by his lover. Worse than that, it looked as if she might be thinking of going back to her husband! Goldthorpe was dealing with the problem by trying to drink himself into oblivion.

The little man was not, romantically speaking, lucky. His own wife had long since packed her bags and run away with a soldier. She said he was crackers, really crackers, and claimed that his behaviour was particularly bad when there was a new moon. Goldthorpe would no doubt have sneered at any mention of her this night and he was certainly not going mad with jealousy about his own wife. The object of his affection was a woman called Marguerite Myers, the wife of a Yorkshireman who among other things was a lay preacher. Goldthorpe had got to know Mrs Myers and her husband at Ossett; one thing had led to another and he and Marguerite had gone down to Norfolk where they were now living in a house at Cobholm in Yarmouth.

Despite that beginning, or indeed perhaps because of it, things had not been going well between them. The relationship was turning sour and earlier that week Marguerite had announced that she was going back to Yorkshire for the weekend to see her husband. Goldthorpe was furious; by turns he had raged and pleaded but neither threats nor declarations of love had made any difference, Marquerite would not be shifted from her determination to return to Ossett.

Now it was Friday night, she had gone, and Goldthorpe was left alone full of jealousy and self-pity and, as the night wore on, frustration. He wanted to strike back, to hurt her, and it was then that an idea came into his warped mind; since she was going to be with her husband, he would repay her in kind – he would get a woman. He drank on until a little before closing time and then went off in search of his woman, an old prostitute called Emma Howe who was usually to be found at a pub called The Great Eastern.

Emma had been a prostitute for most of her life, but she was now sixty-six-years-old and business was naturally somewhat erratic these days. Tonight she had given up, and when the drunken Goldthorpe arrived at The Great Eastern she had already gone home. The early night could have saved her life but Goldthorpe was now determined, and when he heard that she had gone off alone, he set out in pursuit.

The old woman lived in the attractively named Owles Court. By all accounts there was nothing very picturesque about the reality of Owles Court, nor was it, unfortunately, the sort of neighbourhood where drunken men looking for ladies who lived on their own caused any great surprise; when Goldthorpe, unsure where Emma lived, knocked on the wrong door, a helpful neighbour directed him to the right address.

The old girl must have thought her luck was in when the knock at the door came and she found a customer on her doorstep. In fact, quite the opposite was the case; her luck was right out and her end was to be nasty and brutal. She invited the man into her tiny one-roomed home and she took the man into her bed; he used her and then some time in the next hour or so he snuffed out her life, strangling her in her own bed.

In the early hours of the morning Goldthorpe left, shutting the door quietly behind him and stealing away into the night. But rough and poor as it was, Owles Court had at least one grace – it was not a place where comings and goings went unobserved, whatever the hour of day or night. Quietly as Goldthorpe went, he was watched from a blackened window as he left the scene of the murder.

Whether he thought he could get away with it or not was never made clear, but he made no attempt to run for it. He was picked up, very much the worse for drink, in The Great Eastern – Emma's pub – early the next afternoon.

The trial was at Norfolk Assizes and as there could be little argument about the facts of the case, the stage was set for the classical battle which was enacted so many times in these life and death trials. The defence produced its experts to say that Goldthorpe was insane, and the prosecution produced another set of experts who said he was not insane. The jury – good laymen all – made the decision.

The jury went out at twenty past five in the afternoon and in the retiring room quickly reached their first decision … they didn't half fancy a cup of tea!

Now you might have thought that if such a simple request was not possible – and apparently it was not possible – the jury would be quietly told that it was not possible; but that was not

Mr Justice Hilbery's way of doing things. In an act which brought headlines all over the country, he had the whole jury brought back into the courtroom and gave them a public dressing-down in the most pompous and patronizing way possible: 'I understand you have been asking for cups of tea. In the old days it was the formula that a jury was left without food, fire or drink until they agreed on their verdict. I have no intention of applying the full rigour of the law but there are no facilities in this building for making tea.'

He sent them away again, but after that lecture they sorted out all the hours of expert advice, argument and testimony in eight minutes flat! Goldthorpe was guilty.

The little man took it gamely. Asked if he had anything to say before he was sentenced to death, he replied, 'No, only that I thank my counsel and respect the prosecution – they had a rotten job.'

Goldthorpe could obviously not have known it – indeed I suspect he would not have been impressed if he had – but his execution was to be a rather rare event: the debut of a chief executioner. He was to be hanged by a man who had never pulled the lever before, Harry Kirk. It came about because both Albert Pierrepoint and Steve Wade, the only experienced number ones, had accepted an engagement together in Scotland on the date which was fixed for Goldthorpe's execution. As things turned out, the Scottish job was called off, but by then it was too late for the arrangements to be altered; Kirky had been offered and accepted the Norwich job.

I learnt some of this from Pierrepoint when I wrote to him. He replied,

'I am sorry I shall not be with you at Norwich as I had to refuse it as I was engaged in Glasgow, but now they have appealed and I am free on that date but I don't mind, I like to see someone else "have a go".

'I think Harry Kirk will be doing it because Steve should have been with me in Glasgow; and if they get reprieved we get paid so we have to look after them. I shall try and get your name on the Glasgow list first chance I get.'

Pierrepoint was here referring to one of the many differences surrounding executions in England and Scotland. In England if we were engaged for a job and the hanging was cancelled because the man was reprieved, we were not paid a penny; the

Scottish authorities did pay, hence Pierrepoint's desire to 'look after them'. As I read the letter, I thought Pierrepoint was taking it all very cheerfully – but then, being sure of getting paid, he would. There was, however, a word of advice right at the end of the letter: 'I think this is all for now and watch your step very carefully at Norwich.'

I took it to be a warning that Harry was not very experienced, that he had not executed many men before. I had no idea at this time that he had not executed *anyone* before! In blissful ignorance, I was quite unconcerned as I packed my bag for Norwich. I threw in a change of clothing, my shaving kit, a book … and completely on the spur of the moment, my rude scrapbook.

I should say at this point that I like to think I have a sense of humour; I have always enjoyed a tale or two, particularly over a pint. My friends would no doubt describe my sense of humour as earthy – I prefer to call it Rabelaisian. In short, I like a good bawdy joke!

My enthusiasm for the genre led to the start of my collection of verse and ditties. Someone gave me a copy of a poem entitled 'A Farting Contest'. By the standards of today it was laughably innocent and you could now find much worse things in almost any bookshop or newsagents in the land. Nevertheless it was pretty daring for the time and so unusual that an obscure little firm at Holmfirth in Yorkshire could turn a penny or two selling such material. I wrote to them for their catalogue which turned out to be mainly practical jokes – stink bombs, itching powder and the like – but there was a small selection of these rude stories and poems. I bought a couple of them and my collection suddenly started to grow when I circulated them at the pit and people, aware of my interest, donated a few more items. The collection was soon big enough to warrant buying an exercise book in which I stuck them like a scrapbook.

I thought it a harmless enough activity. Had I known the trouble that little book was to cause I would have ripped it into pieces and burnt every last fragment of it. Unaware of the disastrous train of events which it was to set in motion, I thought it might cheer up the evening before the execution.

The early stages of the job went very well. When I arrived in Norwich I went directly to the gaol and found that Kirky was already there. It was a nice, clean, medium-sized prison and the screws were very friendly; they did not have many hangings there and I think many of them were rather curious to see us. The tame screw who was assigned to us was even younger than me and introduced himself, with a laugh, as our 'batman'.

One thing which was unusual was that our quarters were in the same wing as the condemned cell, at a higher level, although it did not register with me just how close we were to the condemned cell. We had a look at Goldthorpe, who was extremely small and seemed very thin, and moved on to the execution chamber. As we went about our preparations Kirky seemed quite relaxed. The prison engineer was lurking about but if it bothered Kirky, he did not let it show. We had been told that Goldthorpe now weighed a 145 pounds and that meant he would have to be given a long drop. As we worked, it became clear that Kirky was planning to give him just over 7½ feet.

To begin with we had a grand night; I can't remember an eve of execution which started better. We had our bottles of beer, Kirky was in fine form and the young screw, once he had got over his initial fear of us, joined in, and was as pleasant company as you could wish for. Kirky was a far more outgoing and talkative person than Pierrepoint and, freed from the sobering presence of 'The Boss', he was very open about the job and told us all sorts of stories, including an account of an amazing assignment which he and Pierrepoint took on for the American forces during the war – a job which far exceeded, in numbers at least, even execution days in Nuremberg.

'We hanged twenty-two yanks in one morning,' he told us. 'They'd got people all over the place who had been sentenced to death, in this country and in Europe. They brought them all to Shepton Mallet in Somerset where they had a big military prison and they brought us in. We did the lot in the one morning.'

'How did you handle that many in such a short time?' I asked him.

'It was a production line,' he replied. 'Shout the name out … bring the man in … read the crime and sentence … drop … down into the pit, check from the doctor … get them off the rope … re-set the trap and adjust the rope … next one …'

'Did you have any trouble?'

'No, we had two bloody great American military policemen on the job just in case, but there wasn't anything serious. They had to carry one or two in because they were almost fainting and couldn't walk but they all stood on their own on the drop.'

'You obviously didn't leave them on the rope for an hour like we do.'

'No,' laughed Kirky. 'Three or four minutes maybe, no more. They wanted them all out of the way that morning and we did them all in the morning.'

'Twenty-two,' I breathed. 'I don't suppose you could even remember all their names.'

'No I couldn't,' he replied, 'but I tell you what I can remember: they paid us for each man. Cash on the nail – in dollars! I've never had such a pocketful of money, and I couldn't spend it!'

Despite the punchline, the account of the mass hangings had a sobering effect on me and the young warder and the atmosphere in the room became very serious for a while … which seemed like a good point to produce my little book and liven up the proceedings! Winking at Kirky, I spoke to the young warder. 'How about a challenge?'

'What?' he asked.

'I have here a book of traditional English erotic poetry,' I continued, brandishing the book. 'Dirty ditties to you, my lad!'

They laughed.

'The challenge is to read one of these – without laughing!'

'You're on!' he responded.

'A shilling says you can't do it,' I told him.

'A shilling says I can!' he laughed.

'Now what shall it be?' I mused. 'Shall I give you "A Farting Contest" …

> I'll tell you a tale that is sure to please,
> Of a great farting contest at Stilton on Peas,
> Where all the best arses parade in the fields,
> To complete in a contest for various shields.

'Shall it be "A Farting Contest"? No, ten verses … that would be unfair! No. It will be "A Corker"!' I declared, settling on one of the items I had bought from the firm at Holmfirth.

It was supposed to be a newspaper critic's review of part of a strongman's act. It was introduced thus:

'At an exhibition held recently in London there was a sideshow in which a man, after putting a cork into an empty cask and blowing into the bunghole, succeeded time after time in blowing the cork out of the cask. A noted London daily newspaper, commenting on this performance, published the following:

'No doubt, a very clever performance, but if the man had put his mouth to the corkhole and blown the cask out of the bunghole, or if he had put his mouth in the cask and blown the bung out of the corkhole, or if he had put the cask into the corkhole and blown the cork out of his mouth, or if he had put the bunghole to his arsehole and blown the cask out of the corkhole, or if he had put his arsehole to his mouth and blown the corkhole out of the bunghole ...,' etc, etc.

I handed the book over to the screw and after composing himself he began to read. His shilling was in trouble almost from the first words. After a couple of lines he was beginning to slow down and there was strain in his voice as he tried desperately not to laugh. He made another line or two, his face working madly as he made a superhuman effort, but when he reached '... or if he had stuffed the bunghole up his arsehole and, blowing the bunghole out of his mouth, pulled his arsehole out of the corkhole ...' he could stand no more and burst out in peals of hysterical laughter. Kirky and I joined in as the book slipped from his helpless fingers.

Suddenly and without warning there was a loud pounding on the floor. The laughter died in an instant. The young screw stiffened, and the smile frozen on his face for an instant before it was wiped away by a sick look of understanding. 'Oh Christ!' he exclaimed. 'Oh bloody hell!'

A feeling of apprehension hit me in the stomach.

'Don't make any more noise,' said the screw, now white-faced, in a whisper. 'It's the condemned cell down below ... they must be knocking on the ceiling with something.'

There was a dreadful hush as we sat in silence for the next two or three minutes waiting for something to happen. I felt quite awful as the implications of what had happened sank in. Our boorish performance was not deliberate, we had not realized the condemned cell was so close to us, but that scarcely seemed to matter. The plain fact was that our laughter had gone ringing round the silent prison so loudly that they could even hear us in the cell where a man was waiting to die in the morning.

I really felt off it as I quietly recovered the damned book and stowed it in my bag. I would not have had such a thing happen for anything and I knew with just a glance at the other two that they must be feeling much the same.

As the minutes ticked away, we heard nothing else and no-one came. That at least was a relief but the cheerful, relaxed atmosphere of the evening was gone completely. I picked up a newspaper and looked at it for a bit, although I did not read a word of it.

Later, just to complete the evening – and to illustrate just how near we were to the condemned cell – we heard Goldthorpe singing, the sound floating up to us as clear as anything.

'At least he's cheerful!' said Kirky humourlessly.

'I'm pleased somebody is,' I replied. 'I wish I'd never brought that bloody book!'

'Well, it's happened now,' said Kirky. 'There's nothing we can do about it.'

I was pleased to go to bed and thankfully soon drifted off, the sound of Goldthorpe, singing away his last night on earth, echoing round the silent prison.

I slept well despite the unfortunate events of the evening, so well that I did not even hear Kirky give his usual snoring performance, which the young screw said had kept him awake half the night. Given the fact that he was waiting for a hanging and given the particular circumstances of this job, I doubt that our friend would have slept very well anyway; I would not think for a moment that he was the first tame screw to lie awake in bed all night listening to the slow breathing of two hangmen.

The events of the previous evening were not mentioned as we got ready to go down to the execution chamber the next morning. Norwich hanged at eight, so we were up and about quite early. Despite the fact that it was Kirky's first job as number one, he seemed relaxed and unconcerned. He had a different style to Pierrepoint, who seemed to take on a grim resolution on execution mornings; but you could sense a determination about him to make this hanging a good one. In the gallows room as we made the final adjustments, he took particular care. Naturally he checked everything I did and there were quietly murmured comments like 'That's right,' or 'That's OK.'

The last job of all was to fasten the loose coils of rope so that the noose was hanging at the right height for Goldthorpe. Kirky gathered the loops together and held them while I tied the packthread. That done, he took one final look around the execution chamber, smiled at me, and then said, 'Well, that's it, young 'un. Let's go and have our breakfast.'

They took us down a little earlier than usual, at five minutes to eight and we were there ahead of the governor and his party. The corridor outside the condemned suite was quiet; the door into both the condemned cell and and the execution chamber were still closed and the guarding screws were just standing around. We waited silently. I put my hand in my pocket to make sure the legstrap was there; it was a recurrent nightmare that I would forget it and find myself walking into an execution chamber, behind a condemned prisoner, with nothing to tie his legs with. A slight noise away to my left caused me to look round and the official party came into view down the wing. As well as the governor, there was the under-sheriff of Norfolk, a small rotund figure with the ruddy complexion of a countryman, and the doctor, along with accompanying warders. Grim-faced they went straight past us in single file and the doctor and the under-sheriff walked straight into the execution chamber. The governor stood with one of the senior prison officers at the entrance. He glanced hurriedly at his watch and then just nodded at us, moving off immediately himself.

I followed Kirky through the door into the condemned cell and found that Goldthorpe was standing talking to a priest. He heard the noise as we came in and turned to look at us. For a moment there was a worried expression on his face but then he said, 'Good morning.'

Kirky replied, 'Good morning,' in a neutral voice which betrayed nothing at all. I just nodded.

As the wide-eyed priest backed out of our way, we went to work. We had his arms strapped with no trouble at all and Kirky walked off, leading the way through on to the gallows. I turned to Goldthorpe who was just standing and pointed him in the direction that Kirky was walking. He followed as quietly as a lamb and although there was a screw on either side of him there was no need for them to assist us.

Goldthorpe was so small that I could see over his head as we went into the execution chamber and I could see Kirky waiting to receive him. Goldthorpe walked right up to him and stopped.

I bobbed down and got my strap round. I was just starting to move clear when Kirky tapped me on the shoulder. He was a fraction slower than Pierrepoint because as I stood clear of the trap. I saw him knock out the safety pins and push the lever over. Goldthorpe plummeted down on that long 7 foot 8 inch drop, there was the boom of the great doors and the man was stopped with a great jerk. I was half-turning to walk to the small trapdoor in the corner when I heard the most spine-chilling sound I ever heard in an execution chamber. From the pit came a snort … and then another snort … and another and another! The rope was still, the head seemed to be over … but there were noises coming from under the hood!

I stood in a state of shock, just rooted to the spot, that terrible sound echoing round the cell. 'It's gone wrong!' I thought. 'Christ – he's still alive!'

I watched, horrified, expecting to see at any moment some movement from the hanging man. He remained still but the breathing sound, now almost like snoring, continued. Kirky, a few feet away across the yawning trap, looked aghast. The governor had a look of utter horror on his face and the little under-sheriff had gone from ruddy red to green.

Somehow I moved; I don't know how I did it, but I turned and then ran for the small trapdoor. As I got it up the doctor came after me. I almost threw myself down the stairs, the sound of Goldthorpe's breathing still coming from under the hood. Down below I grabbed the steps and as I lifted them into position near the hanging feet, the sounds ceased, thank God. I mounted the steps, ripped open Goldthorpe's shirt and got down and out of the way. Hardly had I got clear when the doctor was up with his stethoscope at Goldthorpe's chest.

'He's dead! He's dead!' he announced, and there was no mistaking the relief in his voice.

The doctor put the stethoscope pieces back into his ears and went back to listen to Goldthorpe's chest again. I waited until he had finished and when he got off the steps I went back up and put my hand round the back of the noose. I could put my fingers between the noose and Goldthorpe's neck. The rope was not tight!

'Look!' I said to the doctor, waggling my fingers. He nodded and then added, 'But his neck's broken. He was killed instantly.'

I looked at him but said nothing.

'It was automatic muscular reaction,' he went on, speaking to the people in the upper part of the chamber. 'He was dead.'

The doctor disappeared while I was moving the steps away. By the time I got back into the upper part of the chamber the place was emptying rapidly. The governor, under-sheriff and doctor had already gone, no doubt on their way to stiff Scotches in the office. The prison's chief officer, looking like a man with all the cares in the world on his shoulders, was one of the few people waiting for us; he had to, but he looked as if he would rather be somewhere else. Kirky was quiet and subdued and walked out of the chamber without a word.

There were no Scotches waiting in our quarters and, thank goodness, no sign of our young batman, so we had a few minutes to ourselves. As soon as the door closed behind us I asked, 'What happened?'

'I don't know,' he said with a frown. 'I expect we'll find out in an hour.'

'Did you see me put my fingers between the back of his neck and the rope?'

'Yes, I saw it.'

'The noose wasn't tight!' I exclaimed.

'Yes, I know,' he replied, the worried lines etching his forehead seeming to become even deeper.

I never knew an hour pass so excruciatingly slowly. I sat with a kaleidoscope of thoughts flitting through my mind. What had happened? What had gone wrong? Why had it gone wrong? The doctor said the man had died instantly. Certainly it seemed unlikely that anyone could have been conscious after that drop, even if he had not been killed outright. Seven feet eight, he must have been dead … but it was equally impossible after a fall of that length that the noose could be anything other than tightly round his neck and yet that was the case. How could the rope not be tight? He must have been dead, but the evidence of my own ears was that he was breathing on the rope. How long had it been – a minute, two minutes? No it could not have been anything like that! How long had I stood frozen, listening to the groaning? It seemed like hours but I must have been moving after a few seconds. He could not have been making those sounds for more than half a minute. Heavens, half a minute, that had been long enough!

It was an enormous relief when they came for us after the

hour and I think the two of us could have run to the execution chamber in our eagerness to discover what had gone wrong. There was no sign of the governor or the green under-sheriff; just the engineer officer, the chief officer and a couple of screws to help us get the body down.

We took our measurements and they were precisely what we would have expected them to be; there was no clue there about what had gone wrong.

Kirky came down into the drop and had a look at the corpse, finding he could still insert his fingers between noose and neck. He then went back to the upper level and supervised the two screws as they got the pulley block on the chains. While they worked aloft, I stripped the clothing off the body, leaving only the underclothing on the lower part for decency's sake. The screws lowered a rope sling and I got it into position under the arms of the body. They heaved and lifted it upwards, taking the strain off the hanging rope, and it was then that we discovered what had gone wrong.

Kirky leaned over to take the rope and hood off. He pulled, then he tugged – he could not shift the noose! The linen bag had got caught in the eye of the noose. That thin little bag had stopped the noose going tight around Goldthorpe's neck!

'That was the problem,' he said to the chief officer. 'The bloody hood's jammed in there!'

In fact it was so tightly jammed in that he had the devil of a job to slacken it off. When the noose and bag were off, they lowered the body and one thing was quite obvious: Goldthorpe's neck had been broken; he had been killed outright, as the doctor had said.

Kirky went off to make his report and I went back to our quarters for the last time. It had been a real rotten job from start to finish, I reflected, from the stupidity of last night to the horrific scene in the execution chamber this morning. What a bloody botch-up – and what would be the consequences? I don't know how Kirky explained it in his report but I knew the truth of the matter was that he had made a bad mistake. He had been trying to go too fast, he was trying to show that he was as quick as Pierrepoint. When he put the noose round Goldthorpe's neck he should have seen that the bag was not properly down; maybe he did, maybe he thought it was near enough, and let it go.

As I sat there a screw breezed in. 'Present for you,' he said, handing over a packet of cigarettes. 'He left them for you.'

'Who did?' I asked.

'Goldthorpe!' explained the screw with a grin. 'He said "Give them to the hangman".'

I opened the packet – it contained five unsmoked Woodbines, the last of the little man's wordly possessions.

'Thanks,' I said to the screw. 'I'll pass them on to Harry when he comes back.'

I thought it was only right to offer the fags to Harry. After all, he was the hangman, but I had a pretty good idea who was going to end up with those five Woodbines. I was right too – he would not touch them, he would not even take one of them, so I tucked them into my pocket.

In the normal run of events, Harry and I might well have gone off for a drink at some local hostelry, but neither of us felt like that and the suggestion was never even made. Outside the gaol, he said to me quietly, 'It was bad job wasn't it?'

I did not lie to him. 'Yes – but it could have happened to anyone, Harry.'

He smiled.

'It could have happened to anyone,' I repeated, 'but in any case, he was killed instantly. It didn't make any difference.'

'It was a bad job,' he repeated and we parted. 'See you, young 'un,' were his farewell words, but I was never to see Harry Kirk on a job again.

11   Bribery

After the debacle at Norwich, I thought there was every possibility that my brief career as a hangman was about to come to an early and rapid end. My gloom only deepened about a week later when I spoke to Pierrepoint on the phone; he already knew all about the mess and said authoritatively that Kirky would not be doing another job. The tone of his voice during the brief conversation made it clear that he had no sympathy for his ertswhile friend and colleague, none at all. I was surprised and depressed by that. Pierrepoint did not mention my part in the disaster and I did not tempt fate by asking him.

I smoked Goldthorpe's cigarettes – and enjoyed them too, although it caused a row with Joyce. She asked why I was smoking fags rather than my pipe, and I was foolish enough to tell her where I got them, although not of course the circumstances which had arisen at the execution. She told me it was awful and said I should throw them on the fire. I told her there was no chance of that!

Thirteen days after the Goldthorpe execution I had a brown envelope. The letter was from Manchester Prison and headed '7905 Nicholas Persoulious Crosby … Dear Sir, the above named prisoner is at present in my custody under sentence of death and the time provisionally fixed for the execution is Tuesday the 19th December at 9 a.m.' I was not to be taken off the list!

The following day I had a brief note from Pierrepoint, hastily scribbled in pencil on half a page ripped out of a notebook. It was tucked inside a Christmas Card. He said that he had put a good word in for me.

'The governor of Manchester is expecting a job on the 19th instant, I have told him I would like you to assist if possible, he

142

told me he would do his best, so if you do hear let me know, you can get an early train to Manchester, come up to our place and we will go down in the car. In haste, all the best, hope you are booked for Manchester. Kind regards, Albert.'

Now here was a piece of opportunism if you like! I did not believe for a moment that he had put in a word for me. For a start, jobs were just not assigned on that basis, I knew that for sure. Then there was the matter of the date; his note to me was marked 5th December – the day I had received the letter from the gaol and presumably the day Pierrepoint had been given official notification about the job as well. He had known I was on the job before he wrote! I was beginning to realize that Albert Pierrepoint was not the sort of man to stick his neck out for someone else. Not that I blamed him. After all, things happened to people's necks when they got involved in business they ought not to get involved in!

I entered the date in my diary for six days before Christmas. Naturally I had no intention of disputing with Pierrepoint how I had got the job. If he wanted me to think that he had done me a favour, that was fine by me. Number ones might not be able to get you on jobs but I was sure they could get you off them if they had a mind to – just a couple of words in the right ear after an execution would make sure of that.

The trip to hang Crosby would normally have been one of the shortest I ever made. He was a Leeds murderer and the execution should have taken place at the Armley gaol but at this time they were modernizing a number of execution chambers around the country, to bring them into line with the new standard model. They were working on the Leeds prison and so the condemned prisoner was sent over the Pennines to Manchester.

Crosby was a twenty-two-year-old gypsy who had murdered a young tailoress called Ruth Massey in a particularly brutal way. He had picked her up at a pub called the Brougham Arms Hotel in Leeds. Ironically when they left together just before closing time, Ruth's sister, Miriam, who was in the same bar, told Crosby, 'Think on. Take her straight home.'

Ruth, who was just nineteen, was never seen alive again. Her body was found on waste ground the next day. Her throat had been cut.

Crosby was to give any number of versions of what had happened. He told his cousin that he had walked the girl home with another man and had left them; he claimed that he was walking away when he heard a scream. He told someone else that he had been walking her home when she met someone she knew; he had left them because the other bloke was a big man and he didn't want any trouble. During the trial he claimed that he had been drunk and did not remember leaving the pub. He was asked if he had killed her and he said, 'To be sure I don't know if I did. I don't remember.'

As Pierrepoint suggested, I travelled over on an early train to Manchester on the morning of the eighteenth and then travelled out to The Struggler on the bus, surrounded by people burdened under the parcels and packages of their Christmas shopping. The pub too had a festive air about it, decorated as it was with cards and tinsel. A couple of reporters offered to buy me a drink which with Pierrepoint looking on I had to turn down, more's the pity! A pending execution always brought a few of the newsmen down, but they were not any trouble once they realized that they were not going to get any comment; that at least had been my experience.

The man who made what was undoubtedly the most serious attempt at bribery that I ever faced, just walked up to me in the bar. The proposition was so incredibly outrageous that it took my breath away, although I am a hundred per cent certain that it was made in deadly earnest. I had been at The Struggler for about a quarter of an hour and I was having a drink with a crowd of Pierrepoint's regulars who were clustered around and making a bit of a fuss of me. I had met most of them before on previous trips to the pub. Without really noticing how it happened, I found myself standing next to this chap of about fifty. He called Pierrepoint Albert and seemed to know several of the people in the group, so I assumed that he was one of them.

'Can I have a brief word with you, Syd?' he asked with a cheery smile.

He took just a couple of paces back, but in the crowded and noisy bar that was enough to take us out of earshot of the group.

'You're going to be at the execution tomorrow with Albert,' he said; it was a statement, not a question.

'You know I can't talk about that,' I said brusquely and started to push past him to get back to the others.

'Wait a minute!' he laughed, laying a hand on my shoulder. 'Listen to what I have to say before you rush off.'

The laugh and the friendly manner threw me a bit, I must confess, and I had to step back a pace to get his hand off me, which gave him the chance to carry on.

'Look, I've got a business proposition to make to you,' he said, dropping his voice.

'A business proposition?' I echoed, puzzled. What kind of business proposition could he possibly make to me?

'There would be a big reward – a lot of money,' he said.

Money! The magic word! I waited.

Encouraged by what he saw in my face, he glanced around and moved in conspiratorially. In little more than a whisper he said, 'We want a picture of the hanging.'

It took a second for the enormity of what he was suggesting to sink in. 'A picture?' I gasped. 'A bloody photo?'

'There's a big reward available,' he repeated. 'A very big reward.'

'You're mad!' I told him. 'You're absolutely bloody mad! It's impossible to get a camera in there, let alone take a picture!'

'No it's not,' he replied. 'We will supply you with it. It's a miniature camera, a tiny thing. It's so small you'll be able to wear it on your shirt and it'll be hidden behind your tie until the moment when he goes down – then just press the button. It'll just look as if you're fiddling with your tie.'

What he was saying was so crazy that it left me speechless and then the thought struck me that I was being set-up, it was a joke, someone was trying to take the mickey out of me.

'We're talking about a big reward.' He was still talking. 'The camera will be so small that nobody will see it – that's guaranteed.'

His face was enough to tell me that he was not joking, it was not some prank involving Pierrepoint's mates, this guy was serious! I suddenly disliked this man and the ghoulish thing that he wanted me to do. It was a ludicrously impossible scheme.

'No,' I said curtly, and this time I forced my way past him to rejoin the group at the bar. I really was quite shocked – the idea was just insane, not to mention horrific.

'Anything up, Syd?' asked one of Albert's friends, breaking into my thoughts.

'No,' I replied.

'Ready for another?' he asked, nodding at the empty glass I was holding.

'Yes, please,' I smiled. When he gave me back the refilled glass I asked him, 'By the way, who's the bloke ...?' I looked around the crowded bar but he had gone.

'Which bloke?'

'The one I was talking to a minute ago.'

'Couldn't tell you, Syd. Comes in here now and then, but I don't know who he is. Was he bothering you?'

'No,' I lied. 'It doesn't matter.'

Later I realized that he had been very clever. Nobody had heard him try to bribe me, indeed it would be very difficult to prove he had tried to bribe me. There had been no mention of a sum of money ... just vague talk of a reward. I also had no idea who he was representing; I had assumed that he was a newspaperman but he had not mentioned a newspaper and would any paper have been prepared to print such a picture even if it had one in its possession? The talk of minature cameras clipped to shirts would sound like silly nonsense from a book about secret agents. He had been very clever – he had not even bought me a drink!

I was annoyed about the proposition but I realized that there was not a damn thing I could do about it. Nevertheless, I made a point of mentioning the incident to Pierrepoint when we had dinner in his quarters at the pub a little later, just to cover myself. I did not want any half-heard snatch of conversation getting back to him later.

He knit his brows as he listened to the story. When I had finished he muttered, 'Bloody ghoul!' but he did not suggest that I should take it further and report it.

The Pierrepoints lived in no great style. The room in which we had our dinner was a small sitting-room, with a kitchen attached, at the back of the pub. The most unusual feature of the room, and it struck me as soon as I walked in, was a marvellous row of carved ivory elephants on the sideboard. They were separate pieces, but the trunk of one fitted into the tail of another, the elephants decreasing in size the further down the line they were. The largest was about four inches high and I guess the smallest was just a couple of inches. Pierrepoint told me later that he had been given them on one of his trips abroad.

Anne Pierrepoint was a pleasant plump-faced woman; quite

pretty and very friendly. She chatted away as she prepared the table for our dinner, just pleasantries and generalities. There was no mention of who I was or why I was with them or of death sentences. She treated me as if I was a young friend of Albert's who had dropped in on them from out of town; we could have been off to a football match that afternoon instead of to a prison to hang a murderer.

The dinner she served us was a sort of snack meal, what we would call a brunch these days. I did rather better than Albert – I got a lovely thick piece of gammon and egg, he only got bacon with his egg.

'Just look at that!' he laughed, nodding at my plate and then looking at his own. 'Look at that – and I'm the landlord!'

'I'm not complaining,' I responded.

'I bet you're not!' he replied in mock annoyance.

'Oh hush Albert!' said Anne, with a twinkle in her eye. 'Syd's the guest.'

Anne did not eat with us. Once she had served the meal she disappeared, presumably so that we could talk over our business in private. In fact there was little to say about the Crosby job at this stage. Manchester was one of the gaols where Albert was allowed to take his car inside, which meant that we would be away quickly in the morning, although there was no suggestion that we were likely to be faced with any angry demonstrations over the hanging of Crosby.

After lunch, Pierrepoint showed me some of his souvenirs. First a pair of epaulets which he told me had come from the uniform of Joseph Kramer, the camp commandant at Belsen. They were cloth, black on navy blue, with gold braid.

'How did you get hold of them?' I asked.

'Cut them off after the execution,' replied Pierrepoint.

They were in pristine condition. It looked as if Kramer could have been wearing them yesterday. Spine-chilling. 'I wish I had been at the execution,' I told Pierrepoint, handing the epaulets back.

'Yes,' he said. 'There were a lot of people who made sure they were there for that one – army officers, all sorts of people – and there were a lot more who would have liked to be there. They lined up to shake my hand when it was done.'

Pierrepoint then produced something even more intriguing, his diaries. He brought three books from the sideboard, though

I had the impression there were more. Each volume was leather-bound, about nine inches by six inches. These he did not let me hold but flipped through the pages so that I got just the briefest of glimpses. Each page was a record of an execution: date … prison … name … drop … assistant …

I knew there were hundreds of executions recorded in those books, the names of men, and some women, who had carried out every imaginable crime; some hanged recently, others who had been in their graves for decades. Yet his prized diaries were a disappointment. What he had, so far as I could see, was a technical record of the executions, just a few bare facts covering three or four lines. There was nothing of the crimes they had committed, not even newspaper cuttings. There was nothing of the atmosphere of the executions, no reports of what was said, no comment about the way the condemned man had behaved. I thought the lack of detail was a waste. I told him. 'They're very nice books.'

He said, 'Yes, I had them specially made.'

'Every job in there?' I asked.

'Yes, every one,' he replied, putting the diaries back in the sideboard cupboard and making a point of carefully locking the door.

The next entry Pierrepoint made in the latest edition of his diaries was no doubt as bland as the rest. It would have recorded that Nicholas Persoulious Crosby was hanged at nine o'clock on the morning of 19th December at Manchester Prison. Condemned man's weight, 161 pounds. Height, 5 feet 10 inches. Drop, 6 feet 2 inches. Assistant, S. Dernley. He would also have recorded the fact that there were two trainee hangmen present at the execution, a twenty-seven-year-old man from Doncaster called Harry Smith and a twenty-eight-year-old Scotsman, now living in Manchester, called Leslie Stewart.

Pierrepoint's few lines would not have recorded that Crosby was in a highly excitable state on the eve of the execution, or that the governor was very worried that there was going to be a problem in the morning. One of the screws told me that fourteen relations – 'gypsy types' – had trooped in to see him and say their final farewells during the day. Whether that prolonged leave-taking had upset him I cannot say, but when I asked the screw how it was looking, expecting the usual 'He'll be allright', the officer shrugged his shoulders and told me, 'He's in a bit of a state.'

Further confirmation of these fears about the prisoner came during the evening when Pierrepoint returned from his usual talk with the governor. He said it had been decided that the two new boys were not to go into the execution chamber but were to watch from the door. He explained that the governor was worried about the nervous state of the condemned man and had concluded that the fewer people there were around the trap, the better it would be. It also meant, I thought to myself, that if it came to a scrap there would be fewer people to get in the way.

As it turned out, they were right to be worried about Crosby. He was scared out of his wits and when we entered the condemned cell I think he came very, very close to breakdown and hysteria. He spun round as soon as he heard the cell door open and stood white-faced and wild-eyed, glaring at us as we approached. He had posed immediate difficulties for us, because we had to get his arms strapped behind him. Pierrepoint caught hold of one of his arms and that was almost too much for Crosby. 'There's no need to grab!' he screeched, his voice rising in panic.

He made to go away from Pierrepoint but I moved quickly and grabbed hold of the other arm. As we forced his arms behind him, Crosby caught sight of the strap in Pierrepoint's hand and that set him off again.

'I don't want the straps on … don't put the straps on!'

We totally ignored him, neither of us making any reply. I forced the arm I was holding firmly up behind him.

'Don't put the straps tight!' pleaded Crosby. 'Don't put the straps tight – I've got a bad wrist.'

Of course we never did fasten the straps tightly; it was intended to be only a light restraint except in the direst of emergencies and when Crosby realized it was done, he ceased his struggling.

While all this was going on, the two warders who were there to help us in the event of trouble had moved in very close. They obviously thought we were going to have a fight on our hands and for a moment or two I think it was touch and go, but when Pierrepoint turned and walked off towards the gallows, Crosby turned and after a moment's hesitation began to follow, able to walk unaided into the execution chamber. Once we had him on the mark, Pierrepoint and I were as fast as greased lightning; it was not a situation in which to dilly-dally. I threw myself back. Crosby was down and dead in a split second.

To my left, through the door, I saw the faces staring into the execution chamber ... poor Smith and Stewart! In the corridor they must have heard all the commotion without being able to see what the hell was going on. It must have sounded ten times as bad as it actually was. One look at their faces was enough to tell that it had been quite unnerving ... not a good job for their first experience of executions.

12   Two Days, Three Hangings

At this time there were on average fifteen executions a year in England. 1950 had been a busy year with nineteen; I was present at eight of them. 1951 was to see only fourteen sentences of death carried out and the year was four months old before I was called on; the summons, when it did come, was quite extraordinary. The authorities had decided to hang three men in two days at the same prison!

The situation arose because of the way that London was divided up for execution purposes. Condemned men who had committed their crimes in the area south of the River Thames were hanged at Wandsworth Prison, while Pentonville was the hanging gaol for the area north of the river. The authorities in their wisdom decided to stick to that custom even though it meant that in the spring of the year they ended up with a death row at Wandsworth. There were two men under sentence of death for one crime; they were to swing together. The third man had been sentenced for a completely different crime. The hangings were to be carried out on 25th and 26th April, the double one first.

It was an unprecedented situation, in recent times at least. Added to this was the fact that the double execution was of the two men convicted of the Old Gossy killing. There was enormous controversy and public interest in the case. Some thought the police had got the wrong men; many believed there were others involved in the crime who had not been caught; there was even a body of opinion that the death was not a murder at all.

Old Gossy was the local nickname of Frederick Gosling, a seventy-one-year-old man who despite his great age and growing deafness, still ran a corner grocery shop at Chertsey in Surrey; the sign over the shop door proudly proclaimed: 'Est.

1907'. Early on an evening in January, Old Gossy made a call to his local police station; they had the greatest trouble trying to make out what the excited old man was saying, but it appeared that there had been trouble at the shop and some men had threatened him.

A single policeman was despatched and he found the old man in such a state that he was not able to give a coherent account of what had happened. Fortunately two young schoolgirls were able to help the policeman. They said that they had gone into the shop, heard Old Gossy cry out in the back room and then two scruffy men suddenly appeared and fled. The policeman established that apart from being shaken, Old Gossy had not been hurt and nothing had been stolen. That seemed to be that. The constable went back to make his report.

At nine o'clock the next morning the man who delivered milk to the shop found the door locked and no sign of the proprietor. That was most unusual, so he went round to a side-door which he found was open. Now thoroughly alarmed, he crept into the house and found the old man in the bedroom. He was tied to the bed, gagged … and dead.

The pathologist's report showed that Mr Gosling had died through suffocation because he had been clumsily gagged with a duster. Reporters briefed by murder-squad detectives later that morning were told that it was a senseless and unnecessary killing; by no stretch of the imagination could the old man have posed any sort of threat to anyone.

The story which lay behind the death of Old Gossy was a tale of greed and stupidity and sheer incompetence. As the story was played out in public, it was to display betrayal in the sordid world of minor crime, thief accusing thief in desperate attempts to escape the noose, and a man giving evidence which could only send his brother to the gallows.

Old Gossy was eccentric about money. He did not have a till in the shop but kept his cash in a back room. Even a sale involving a one-pound note meant he disappeared through the back to get the change. The secretive behaviour led to rumours that he was rich, and there were soon stories that he kept 'all his money' hidden somewhere on the premises. The idle chatter soon spread far enough for it to be picked up by highly-tuned and dishonest ears.

The man who planned the robbery was a twenty-seven-year-old labourer called Frederick Brown from nearby Ashford. He first involved his older brother, Joseph, aged thirty and together they recruited a lorry-driver called Edward Smith, another thirty-year-old; he had not been involved in crime before but was tempted by the Brown brothers, who said they could put him on to some easy money if he was prepared to join them on a job. The plan was simple: Frederick Brown was to keep watch outside Old Gossy's shop while Joseph Brown and Smith were to enter and carry out the robbery. Inside they would buy something small and give the old man a pound note; when he went to get the change, he would lead them to the money. As soon as Old Gossy, followed by Smith and Brown, went into the back room. Frederick Brown was to enter the shop and lock the door so that no-one could get in while the robbery was in progress.

At six o'clock one evening the plan was put into effect and it came within an ace of success. When Old Gossy was given the pound note he duly disappeared into the back room; from the doorway Smith and Brown watched him go to a bureau in a corner and open a drawer. The two robbers were entering the back room when there was a racket from the shop doorbell. Brown looked over his shoulder, expecting to see his brother. Instead there were two girls coming in – and no Frederick! The bell had also attracted the attention of the half-deaf old shopkeeper who turned from the bureau, saw Smith and Brown, and started shouting his head off.

'Keep him quiet!' snapped Brown.

Smith moved over, grabbed hold of the old man, and tried to get a hand over his mouth, but Old Gossy carried on struggling and Smith's nerve broke. 'Let's get out!' he urged.

The two men ran for it, bursting out of the back room, past the girls and out of the shop.

When they were eventually able to question their 'lookout man' to find out what had gone wrong, Frederick claimed that someone he knew had come up to him in the street and started talking; it had been impossible for him to get inside the shop and lock the door. The police, meanwhile, were now getting their confused call from the shopkeeper.

About the story this far there is no dispute. All three men were to admit the attempted robbery and their part in it. What happened next is quite a different matter. Far from being scared off by the close call at the shop, some appetites had merely been whetted and someone decided to go back and try again – that night.

Old Gossy was woken in his bed and trussed up. His legs were bound to the foot of the bed, his jacket pulled down so that he could not move his arms, and his tormentors tried to force him to say where he kept his money. It took a long time to get it out of Old Gossy … thirteen cigarette ends were found in the hearth. Eventually either the old man gave in or perhaps the raiders struck it lucky, but the safe key was found in his trouser pocket and the safe was cleared out. It is thought there was between forty and sixty pounds in notes and silver. Before they left, Old Gossy was gagged; an action which was to open the road to the gallows.

For a week the murder squad found their investigation was going nowhere fast, but then they had some lucky breaks. First there was a tip that it was 'the Brown brothers' who had done the job. They did not even know which of the Brown brothers they were after, but by a fluke they happened to pick Frederick up first, and he turned out to be the vital weak link in the criminal chain. Unaware of how little the police had, Frederick cracked. 'All right,' he told them, 'I arranged it. It's not George, it's my other brother Joe.'

Frederick and Joseph were put before magistrates on a holding charge of assaulting Mr Gosling with intent to rob him, but the police case was still looking fragile. When they put the Brown brothers in an identity parade, before twelve witnesses who had been around Old Gossy's shop at the time of the first raid, no-one recognized them.

At some stage a deal was done and Frederick really started throwing everyone to the wolves to save his own skin. He fingered Smith, gave what he claimed was a full confession, agreed to testify in a murder trial which he knew could send the other two to the gallows, and the charge against him was dropped.

Smith and Joseph Brown went on trial at the Kingston Assizes accused of murder. The prosecution's star witness was Frederick. In the witness box he admitted formulating the original plan and confessed that he had been involved in the first attempt to rob the shopkeeper but said that he had not gone back in the night. He claimed that he was unaware that Smith and his brother were planning to return until the next morning when they told him they had done the job. They said they had tied up the old man but he had been all right.

The defence mounted a massive counter-attack on him but he stuck doggedly to his story. He had not gone back to the shop. The defence produced a surprise witness, a man who was serving six months in Brixton gaol, who claimed to have had a conversation with Frederick while he was being held on remand there. The prisoner swore that Frederick had revealed he planned the job and that he had gone back with a friend, not Smith and Joseph. 'He said his solicitor told him to keep quiet and he was going to be discharged.'

Smith and Joseph fought for their lives and both of them pointed the finger at Frederick sitting, a free man, a few feet away from them in the courtroom.

The jury was out for three and a half hours before the verdict of guilty was returned. Brown's mother collapsed in the courtroom and had to be taken by ambulance to hospital when the judge, Mr Justice Parker, pronounced the sentence of death.

The governor of Wandsworth Prison wrote to me a few days later, on 8th March, offering me an engagement in respect of Smith. It was a preliminary letter; the date of the execution had not been fixed. Nine days later I had another letter from Wandsworth. I opened the envelope expecting further details of the Smith job, and found to my surprise that it was another invitation to accept an appointment, this time in respect of a different condemned prisoner, James Virrels. Again it was a preliminary letter, and no date had been fixed for the execution.

Virrels, a fifty-five-year-old labourer, was to go to the gallows for the gruesome murder of his landlady ... following a row about jam sandwiches! He was engaged to the lady, Mrs Alice Roberts, a widowed mother of five young children, and a date had been set for the wedding in Worthing, where they lived. According to Virrels, the trouble started when he complained that she had been sending him to work with only bread and jam to take with him for lunch. There ensued a blazing row and he claimed that she came at him with a dagger. Whether that was true or not, the knife ended up in his hand and he stabbed her with it. He then got hold of an axe and used that on her as well. Leaving the body of Mrs Roberts in the bloodstained kitchen, where it was discovered by her eldest son when he came home from school at lunchtime, Virrels fled to his brother's house where he announced, 'I've committed a murder.'

Virrels was duly found guilty of murder and sentenced to death. His final plea was rejected by the Court of Criminal Appeal in April; the same sitting rejected the pleas of Smith and Brown. Three days later two letters were on their way to me from Wandsworth Prison. The first explained that Smith and Brown were to be hanged at nine o'clock on the 25th, the second that Virrels was to be executed at the same time the following morning.

The three days in London were to be the peak of my career as a hangman. It seems strange looking back on it from this television age of instant news coverage, with pictures and interviews of almost everything anywhere in the world, but though there was enormous public curiosity about executions and hangmen, people actually learnt very little about us and they did not even know what we looked like; the odd fuzzy picture of Pierrepoint in a newspaper was the most that they got. On this trip, I was to discover just how great was the interest in us and our job.

The day before the Smith and Brown hanging I got myself down to London in time to meet Pierrepoint off his train at Euston. We took a taxi and Pierrepoint told the driver to take us to Barney Finnegan's. 'I've arranged to meet someone there,' he explained.

On the way, he told me that the other men on the job were to be my old mate Harry Allen and another man, from Manchester, also called Harry Allen. They were not related; it was just a strange coincidence that there were two men of the same name on the list and they both happened to be on this job. The Manchester Harry Allen, whom I had not met before, was one of the most senior men on the list.

Barney Finnegan's was a pub run by an Irishman. It was a favourite watering hole of Pierrepoint's and he invariably headed there at some time when we were working in London. When we arrived I discovered that the 'someone' he had arranged to meet was Bob Fabian, then the most famous detective in the whole country – 'Fabian of the Yard' – who had a reporter from the *Empire News* in tow. I must confess that I was a little in awe of the great detective. I had read so much about him and here he was actually standing talking to me! In fact,

Fabian was friendly and very easy to chat to. Pierrepoint and he had been friends for years; the conversation was light and jokey, with lots of stories and leg-pulling, and talk between them of mutual acquaintances. I did not say much; I was just pleased to be there and to be included in the group; this was, after all, why I had become a hangman.

With the landlord and half the bar staff dancing attendance on our little group, nothing was said about the job. The reporter tried to raise the subject and remarked to Pierrepoint, 'They're working you hard this week, Albert!'

I held my breath and waited to see what happened next. When the response came it sounded friendly. 'Oh aye … 'nough said.'

The smile stayed on Pierrepoint's face but the eyes were icy. It killed the line of inquiry stone dead. The reporter looked slightly uncomfortable and had better sense than to go on.

By now news of our presence had gone round the pub. Indeed, it felt as if the word had gone round the adjoining streets. Heads started popping round the doors, gawping, and disappeared as quickly and mysteriously as they appeared. I could imagine what was being said in the other rooms: 'Pierrepoint and his assistant are in there with Fabian! Pierrepoint's on his way to hang those two for the Old Gossy murder!'

After about an hour Fabian had to go off and we were ready to move on somewhere else, so our little group broke up. Pierrepoint said that we would be going to Scotland Yard in the morning to see 'Whack' Daws, head of the Flying Squad. One of the barmen jumped to order us a taxi and we continued on our way.

Pierrepoint was a wonder; he seemed to me to know half the pub landlords in London and was guaranteed the most amazing reception wherever he went. He normally stuck to houses where he knew the people, although very occasionally we went into a new place and then we were just two chaps standing at the bar having a quiet pint. There was very little chance of us being recognized; none at all in my case. Even though Pierrepoint's picture was sometimes in the paper, it never looked anything like him and no-one ever came up to us in those circumstances.

At the next pub the landlord was ecstatic when we walked in. He all but jumped over the bar in his eagerness to greet us. 'Nice to see you Albert!' he beamed. 'What are you having?'

We stood talking to him for a few minutes, drinking our beer, and then the landlord beckoned over one of his regulars. 'Hey Tom, come here a minute.'

Tom, a thin, fair-haired man in his late thirties or early forties, wandered over.

'This is a friend of mine from Manchester,' said the landlord, nodding at Pierrepoint. 'Shake hands with him.'

Tom put his hand out and Pierrepoint, who obviously knew what was coming, took hold of it with a friendly smile.

The landlord then laughingly announced to his friend, 'You're shaking hands with Albert Pierrepoint – the public hangman!'

Poor Tom! I just had to laugh at the look on his face. He stood there with his mouth half open, frozen, unable to withdraw his hand or to look away from the cool, blue eyes which surveyed him. Then for some unaccountable reason he started to blush!

The landlord seemed to think it was a great joke, until Pierrepoint said to him, 'He looks like he could do with a drink,' and nodded at Tom's almost empty glass.

So to the landlord's discomfort, Tom got a free pint and with the time moving on we decided that we had better head for the prison.

'Will you be back tomorrow?' asked the landlord.

'Yes, see you tomorrow,' replied Pierrepoint casually. The landlord beamed.

Outside Pierrepoint told me, 'Bugger him! We're not going there tomorrow.'

I could imagine the landlord talking to all his cronies and the word going round that Pierrepoint and his assistant would be in the pub tomorrow after the Old Gossy hangings. The place would be packed to the doors. Tomorrow the joke would be on him.

We met the two Harry Allens at Wandsworth. The Manchester Harry Allen seemed a cheerful type, if a little flamboyant; I could scarcely believe the bow tie! He was friendly enough, in a condescending way that announced that he was the senior assistant and we were mere newcomers.

Having now been to seven prisons, I thought I had seen it all, but the execution chamber at Wandsworth was something else! It was of the same proportions as all the rest, but everything – and I mean everything – was polished and spotless and glinting.

Even the floor was varnished and shining. Most unbelievable of all, the ropes for the warders to hang on to if they had to hold the man up during the execution, had pretty woven sallies on the ends like church bell ropes. They were beautiful coloured things; everywhere else made do with simple knots on the ends of the ropes. I never saw anything like it at any other prison.

Before we rigged we had a look at the condemned men – Smith and Brown, that is; we saw no sign of Virrels and no-one made any reference to him. Smith was in the condemned cell nearest to the drop. As we worked, it became clear that both men were to get drops of over 7 feet: 7 feet 3 for Smith and 7 feet 1½ inches for Brown. I was to go for Smith with Pierrepoint.

The controversy surrounding the Old Gossy case was still raging. The *Sunday Despatch* had carried a story that Frederick Brown had been forced to quit his job and leave his sister's home in Ashford after threats. He was trying to start a new life where he was not known and he told the newspaper that when his new workmates talked about the murder trial in the canteen, he just kept quiet. His sister, who had stood by him, had been compelled to abandon her job in a department store; she had also been threatened in the street and told that she would be waylaid some night.

'I know what people are saying behind my back,' he told the *Despatch*. 'They believe I hanged by brother to save my own neck. It's just not true.'

Despite the circumstances there was no discussion about the rights or wrongs of the case in our group that night. That was a problem which had been dealt with by other people. Smith and Joseph Brown were to hang in the morning; there was no point in talking about it.

Smith went to the scaffold with considerable bravado. He was waiting for us when we entered the cell and offered no resistance when we pinioned his arms but he snapped at me when I tried to guide him. Pierrepoint had turned to lead the way through the door into the execution chamber and I took hold of Smith's arm to make him follow, but he growled, 'Leave me alone – I'll walk on my own!'

The two screws started to move in on Smith but when I let go of his arm he turned and walked quickly through. On the trap I strapped his legs and was just straightening up when Brown was brought in. The senior Harry Allen stood back and the other Harry did his part with the legstrap and they both went down. It was quite a quick job for a double.

Just over an hour later, outside the prison gates, Pierrepoint and I said goodbye to the two Harry Allens. Their job was done and we were heading into the town. I was never to work with my friend Harry again as things turned out.

Our first stop was in Soho where Pierrepoint wanted to call at Jack Soloman's gymnasium, or boxing training academy as I believe it was called. I have never been even remotely interested in the ring but there was a big fight coming up, some British Empire title or other, and Pierrepoint wanted tickets. We went up some stairs and met a chap with an enormous cigar in his mouth. 'Bloody 'ell – Albert Pierrepoint,' he spluttered. 'What do you want?'

'I'm after a couple of tickets for the fight,' responded Pierrepoint. 'Ringside tickets!'

'You'll be bloody lucky!' laughed the man with the cigar. 'They went weeks ago.'

'Two tickets,' smiled Pierrepoint, and then added with mock menace, 'or you'll be next!'

'OK, OK,' said the cigar man, hands raised in submission. 'Can you drop back tomorrow?'

'Yes,' said Pierrepoint.

'Who are you bringing?' asked the cigar.

'Never you mind,' replied Pierrepoint.

I mention this last because a while later I almost split my sides when I saw a photograph of Pierrepoint in the *Picture Post* at a fight. The caption said something like 'Albert Pierrepoint and his wife at the fight'. I do not know who the woman was that Pierrepoint was sitting with; it sure as hell was not Anne Pierrepoint! When I asked him about it later, he muttered darkly that they had made a mistake and he was going to sue them, but I never heard any more about it.

Pierrepoint having fixed up his tickets, we moved on to Scotland Yard where we asked the policeman on duty at the desk if we could see Mr Daws. When the policeman asked who we were, Pierrepoint produced a card – that did the trick!

'Whack' Daws – Detective Superintendent Daws – turned out to be a really friendly, jovial chap with the most enormous ears; he also had a huge reputation for criminal detection and had figured in some very famous cases. He was delighted to see us and we had only been in his office for a few minutes when he said, 'Do you want to see some gold?'

'Yes,' we replied.

'Well keep your bloody hands in your pockets', he told us, 'and don't take them out until you leave!'

He took us to a room; it was like an Aladdin's cave. There was a table which must have been the best part of twenty feet long, absolutely covered with gold – coins, medallions, jewellery. They had made a big arrest and it was all loot, from various robberies, which had been recovered; each piece was identified with a tag. The surface of the table looked yellow. Heaven knows what the value of it must have been.

We were allowed to look as much as we wanted but he would not let us pick up any of the items for a closer look. 'You're joking!' he said. 'I'm not letting you two get your hands on it!'

I really hoped that I would get a chance to have a look around the black museum at Scotland Yard, the place where they keep all the weapons and implements used in murders and other notorious crimes, but when I got round to asking, Pierrepoint said the time was getting on and we should be on our way. Daws said he would take me another time, but I never did get to see it.

Lunch was a sandwich and a drink at yet another establishment where Pierrepoint was known and got a warm welcome, and then it was time to return to carry out the second part of our engagement. It seemed strange to be in exactly the same quarters, going through exactly the same routine, but this time just the two of us.

At fifty-five, Virrels seemed an old man to me; indeed, he was the oldest man that I ever helped to hang. He looked absolutely terrified when we went for him the next morning. His eyes were staring wildly, and I thought he was having trouble walking to the gallows, although he did manage on his own. It slowed us down and the execution took twelve seconds. When I stripped the corpse later I discovered that he had messed himself. I mention this unsavoury fact because of the stories which circulate about hangings; I have been told by people that condemned men always lose control of themselves at the end. I can honestly say that of all the executions I attended, this was the one and only occasion that it happened.

I parted from Pierrepoint when we got out of the prison. He

was off to pick up his boxing tickets before, no doubt, another round of socializing. I could have gone with him but I just wanted to get back to Nottinghamshire. I put it down to being tired; it did not occur to me until much later that it might be something else. I was walking through the marketplace at Mansfield when I passed two pretty young girls. They were a couple of steps behind me when I heard one of them say, 'Did you see that man – what terrible eyes!'

13 One for the Record Books

There was never a shred of doubt that the British public fully supported the use of the death penalty. Murderers deserved to be hanged and the sooner the better ... that was the view of the great majority of people. Nevertheless, I have to admit that it was unusual to find a condemned man with those views.

James Inglis became a date in my diary one sunny afternoon in April. That was when he stood in the dock at Leeds Assizes in the final, electric moments of his trial for murder. Mr Justice Gorman was about to send the twenty-nine-year-old Scotsman to the gallows, but before he pronounced the words of sentence he asked, 'Have you anything to say?'

Inglis looked at him for a moment and then replied, 'I've had a fair trial from you and the members of your court. All I ask now is that you get me hanged as soon as possible.'

The chilling words brought an audible gasp from some of the spectators in the public gallery. None of the people in that courtroom would know, but Inglis was to get that last request. Never was a man hanged so quickly!

Inglis' story is worth the telling, if only because it was so typical of many of the criminals who were hanged. The murder was particularly brutal and cruel but above all, it was insanely pointless.

The setting for the story was the seedy backstreets of the port of Hull, the city on the River Humber whose prosperity was based on the great fleet of deep-sea trawlers which roamed the Arctic fishing grounds of Iceland and Norway and Greenland. Now *there* was a job which made even mining look like a soft option; the fisherman's life was one of long weeks at sea, working on the open decks of small ships in some of the worst waters in the world. I have no doubt that most of the trawlermen were as steady as anybody else but inevitably it was the others that we read about – the three-day millionaires who arrived back in port with three weeks' money burning a hole in their pockets. For a little time there were the bright lights ... taxis everywhere ... drinks for everyone ... meals ... dancing ... and then it was over as quickly as it had begun. Broke, they made their way back to their ships on some cold Humberside dawn to catch the tide and sail away to the northern fishing grounds once more.

At the bottom of the pile there were drunkenness and prostitution, a twilight world with few markers or rules, and it was into this stagnant backwater that Inglis washed up. The army had brought him to Hull during the war but had him committed to a mental hospital because of his behaviour. When he was released just before Christmas in 1945, he stayed on for the simple reason that he had nowhere better to go. He had a string of jobs; a few days labouring here, a few days there, a week at a factory; never staying for long, always being sacked or throwing his hand in and walking out. He lived in lodgings, again never for long, always moving on or being moved on.

At the time that our interest in him begins, Inglis had been working for a few days at a shipyard in Hessle, on the outskirts of Hull, and was lodging at a small red-brick terraced house in Barmston Street in the eastern part of the city, a stone's throw from the wharves and quays of the brown river which give Hull its name. The landlord was Herbert Bell, a barman who lived in the house with Amy Gray, a woman who throughout the events which were to follow was described as his 'housekeeper'. Inglis had been there a few weeks, even though they had been told that he had attacked a woman before he came to them. They had found him such a quiet, inoffensive man that they had dismissed the stories. It was a bad mistake.

It would be difficult to say what was important to Inglis, obviously it was not work or home; food likewise was a minor matter and meals were as often as not brought home wrapped in newspaper from one of the local fish and chip shops. It really came down to drink, on which he spent most of his money in the pubs around the city centre, and sex, which he usually paid for.

Drink and paid-for-sex were also important to Alice Morgan, the other principal player in this tragedy, although she had known better things in her life. Alice had been born on what must have been the fringes of the middle classes in a fishing port like Hull. She was the daughter of a trawler skipper and at the age of twenty married a rich if not entirely respectable man, who operated as a moneylender. The marriage produced two children but ended in divorce, and after that Alice slid into a world of booze, prostitution, and friendships with men like James Inglis. She now lived in a small house in a terrace off Cambridge Street, behind the Paragon railway station and only a few hundred yards from the city centre.

Alice was now fifty years old but still slim and attractive. Her life was an endless round of drinking in the pubs and bars of the area and of numberless, nameless 'chaps' who bought her drinks, paid her five pounds to go to bed with her and later went on their way, without Alice or anyone else living in Cambridge Street being very concerned. Despite her lifestyle, Alice was by all accounts a pleasant woman, known to all and sundry in the area, and her neighbours took the view that what she did was her own affair. She was certainly not the only lady in the locality to have an unusually large number of gentleman friends.

In this world of free and easy, transient relationships, these two pieces of flotsam and jetsam came together early in the new year. The actual circumstances of their first meeting are unknown; it seems likely that they came across each other in one of the pubs around the Anlaby Road and that Inglis became one of Alice's customers. For about three weeks they were regularly out and about together, although whether the relationship progressed is a matter of conjecture. It seems likely that they viewed it differently. Inglis, if he understood what sort of life Alice was living, may have thought that he was different to her other men; he viewed her as a friend, perhaps even as a girlfriend. Alice did not regard him as being in any way special; so far as she was concerned Inglis was just another in the long line of men who gave her money.

This sordid, unimportant little affair exploded into front page headlines in the first few days of February. Ironically, if Inglis was to be believed, he was about to quit Hull. On the morning of Thursday 1st February, he went in to work at the shipyard in Hessle, gave them what he described as 'one minute's notice' and walked out. He had only been in the job since Monday. He told the foreman that he had domestic trouble and was returning home to Scotland. In fact it was an impulse decision, seemingly made on the bus journey between home and work. After leaving the shipyard, he went back to his lodgings in Barmston Street, washed, changed into his best clothes, and returned to collect his money – two pounds and four shillings.

With money in his pocket, Inglis headed not for Scotland but to the nearest pub and there he stayed until closing time when they turned him out. At a loose end, he took a bus back into the centre of Hull and walked round to see if Alice was in. It was her unlucky day – she was. Inglis wanted to carry on drinking and asked Alice if she could get them some booze; nothing loath she walked round to the Victoria Vaults but by this time it was four o'clock, they were closed, and they were not prepared to sell, even to a good customer like Mrs Morgan.

The pubs opened again at six o'clock and Charles Smith, licensee of the Queen's Head on Walker Street, had hardly got his doors open before the two of them were in there. They were his only customers and he stood chatting to them for a few minutes. Inglis was still maintaining that he was about to leave Hull but he was now claiming that he was about to 'rejoin' the Foreign Legion, and produced some papers which he said were the reply to his application. As more people came into the pub, Charles Smith moved away, Inglis and Alice had a drink with a friend of hers, and they then moved on to the Victoria Vaults, the drinking shop just around the corner from Cambridge Street. There they met Hannah Short, another 'housekeeper', who had known Alice for about twenty years. At about eight o'clock, Inglis suggested they go home. They walked out of the Victoria Vaults, turned right along Anlaby Road, turned into Pease Street and arrived in Cambridge Street. As they walked, they passed Beatrice Ward, the last friend to see Alice Morgan alive.

In the small house Inglis and Alice had a furious row. Inglis, with little money to begin with, had been spending on beer all day, not least with her, and he was now just about broke. He could not afford her. Alice knew she could get five pounds off a chap tonight and she told him so. Inglis went berserk. His fists smashed into her face and body, ripping skin and breaking bones. Alice crashed against the furniture as she collapsed. Inglis attacked her where she fell. Soon there was blood everywhere, but he went on and on and on …

At the Victoria Vaults, an hour or so later, Hannah Short was still enjoying her night out. She looked up as the door into the bar opened and in walked the man she had seen go off with Alice.

'Where is she?' Hannah asked.

'I took her home,' replied the man. 'She was sick with her shoulder and I put her to bed.'

Hannah nodded and said no more to him. James Inglis bought himself another drink and then quietly left by the back way.

Herbert Bell and Amy Gray were both in when Inglis arrived back at the house in Barston Street. He seemed quite his normal self and they did not notice anything unusual about him. Amy asked if he had eaten anything and when he said that he had not, she went out and brought him some fish and chips. Inglis ate them and went to his bed, but he could not sleep. Each time he closed his eyes he saw before him the battered and bloodstained face of the woman he had just killed.

The body of Alice Morgan was to lie undiscovered on the bloodstained couch for the whole of the next day and the following morning; thirty-six hours. A ten-year-old boy who ran errands for Alice went into the house on that Friday afternoon; getting no response when he knocked, he pushed the door and found it was not locked. He walked into the sitting-room, where the curtains were still drawn, and in the darkened room saw a shape on the settee. Alice was covered with a blanket and piles of clothing. All he could actually see were her bare feet sticking out. Mercifully, the lad assumed she was asleep and quietly left the house.

There was more to come though. At about the time that the boy was in Alice's house, on the other side of the city Inglis was going berserk again, this time at his lodgings in Barmston Street.

Early in the day, Inglis had left the house and spent several hours wandering aimlessly on the streets on Hull. Finally, in the middle of the afternoon, he returned to his lodgings where he found Amy Gray in the house on her own, and very concerned that he had given up his job. She tried to ask him questions. Why had he left the job? What was he going to do? What about money? Inglis did not seem to understand what she was saying to him and just rambled in a strange, nonsensical way. Amy pressed on with her questions about money and then Inglis asked her to go upstairs and look in a box on the dresser in his bedroom. She did as he said and was just opening the box when blows rained down on the back of her head. Amy crashed to the floor and then he started to strangle her ...

On his way out of the house, Inglis took an iron bar to the gas meter, where he got a few shillings, and he filched a few pence that he found in Amy's handbag. She was found an hour and a half later.

On Saturday morning postman Harry Thomas was trying to deliver a registered parcel at Alice Morgan's house without any success. He got no reply on his first visit, so he went away and returned at noon to try again. There was still no answer when he knocked and so he went next door. The neighbour said it was strange, and walked round with the postman. She pushed the door open and crept into the darkened living-room. She saw there was someone on the couch but became frightened and ran out.

Harry went into the room and spoke to the bundle on the settee. There was no response. The postman moved some of the clothing, and found himself looking at a smashed, bloody face; the tongue protruded through the teeth. He ran out of the house to raise the alarm.

Alice's face was so pulped and battered that the postman thought he was looking at the body of a man. The first examination of the body at the scene revealed to detectives a sickening catalogue of injuries. That it was a woman became clear when the pile of clothing was removed, for Alice was naked from the waist down. There was a silk stocking tied so tightly round the neck that it was embedded in the flesh. The tongue was out of the mouth like a balloon. The face was covered with clotted blood and there were enormous bruises all over the body.

The full extent of Alice Morgan's horrific injuries were to become clear at the morgue when the police surgeon, Dr Watts Waters, got to work. When he cleaned the dried blood away, he found there were cuts to her left eye, chin and ear. As she had been strangled, five of her teeth had penetrated her tongue. She had a stab wound in the head, probably done with something like a hat-pin. The initial attack had been so ferocious that almost all the bones of the face had been literally pulverized. Dr Waters reported that the actual cause of death was strangulation and multiple fractures of the skull. He said he had never seen anything like it.

While Dr Waters' examination was still in progress, the Chief Constable of Hull, Sydney Lawrence, was telling the reporters from the *Hull Daily Mail* that at this stage they had no clue as to who the murderer might be. In reality, it was quickly established that the man they were hunting was James Inglis, already being sought for the attack on Amy Gray.

For the next twelve hours the police turned Hull upside-down and inside-out in the race to get to Inglis before he struck again. Every available man was called in, every other task subordinated to the hunt to find the homicidal maniac who was on the loose in the city. The town was flooded with officers; every pub and bar was checked, every face in every crowd scrutinized that Saturday afternoon, but as the hours ticked away, still there was nothing. Checks on the railway station, bus stations, even the ferry which could have taken Inglis across the water to Lincolnshire, drew blanks. It was as if he had simply vanished into the air.

For a time the city centre became quiet as the stores closed their doors and the shoppers went home, but then people flooded back in for their evening out. The police operation continued remorselessly and finally, a little after eleven o'clock, headquarters got the news ... they had him!

At the end, Inglis was pathetic and grovelling. They ran him to ground at Victoria Mansions, the Salvation Army hostel for homeless down-and-outs, in Great Passage Street, a stone's throw from Cambridge Street. He blurted out a confession as soon as Detective Inspector James Cocksworth identified himself.

'I knew you'd be coming,' he said. 'You know – Cambridge Street. I done it. I killed a woman.'

Cocksworth started to formally caution Inglis as the law required. He said, 'This morning I saw the body of a woman named Alice Morgan at 4 Eton Terrace, Cambridge Street. She had been strangled with a stocking and had multiple injuries to her face ...'.

Cocksworth got no further. Inglis interrupted, 'Don't tell me any more about it, please sir. I have been walking ever since. I'm glad you've come.'

Cocksworth told Inglis he was being arrested. He replied, 'Yes, I know. I went barmy. Please don't tell me any more about it. I did it.'

In fact there was even more on Inglis's conscience – Amy Gray had not been mentioned – and while arrangements were being made to take him in, he found himself alone with a detective constable. Inglis unburdened his mind. 'You had better go to Barmston Street as well. There's another one there. I went mad there too.'

The detective started to caution Inglis, but he brushed the warning aside and burst out, 'Tell me, is she dead?'

The detective replied, 'No, she's not dead.'

Inglis said, 'Thank God. I thought there were two.'

Amy had been more fortunate than Alice Morgan. She came round some time after Inglis had left the house and dragged herself downstairs and into the street where she raised the alarm. She was taken to hospital where it was found she had wounds to her chin, face and lips. There was also damage to her right cheekbone and there had been an attempt to strangle her.

Inglis made no appeal and so the execution was set for Tuesday 8th May. Hangings were no longer carried out at Hull Prison; Inglis would normally have been sent to Leeds but the execution suite there was still not in operation and he was sent to Manchester.

Unusually, on this job I actually knew what our man looked like even before we got to the prison; the newspapers had taken a perfect close-up photograph of Inglis arriving for one of the court hearings, handcuffed to a detective – there had been none of the usual business of rushing him in the back way with a blanket over his head. But good though the picture was, the short interval of time in the condemned cell had taken its toll on him; when we looked at him through the spyhole he seemed thinner and a lot more bald. Nevertheless, he appeared strikingly cool for a man spending his last day on earth. He was playing cards with the two screws, talking and laughing, seemingly quite unconcerned about his situation.

As we got to work Pierrepoint said that he now weighed just 139 pounds, and he was planning to give him a drop of eight feet, the longest I had ever seen.

That night Albert dropped a real bombshell. 'By the way,' he announced casually, 'your friend Harry Allen's finished.'

'No! Harry from Birmingham?' I checked.

'Yes.'

'Sacked?' I asked, always being one to fear the worst.

'No, he quit voluntarily,' said Albert. 'Apparently his boss told him that ice-cream and hanging don't mix. Told him he was going to get the sack if he carried on with it.'

'So he decided to pack this job in.'

'Yes,' replied Pierrepoint.

'First Kirky, now Harry!' I exclaimed. 'There'll soon be nobody left.'

'There'll always be somebody left,' replied Pierrepoint with a grim smile.

I knew he was right. There would always be somebody – not least him. If it came to a decision between hanging and a regular job I had no doubts which he would choose! How about me? What if the pit manager decided that welding and hanging didn't mix? Now there was a question!

Pierrepoint warned me that the High Sheriff of Yorkshire was to be present at the execution in the morning. Now this was unusual – the High Sheriff, not one of his officials. The high sheriff of a county was always some landowning member of the gentry who served for just a year in the job after his name had been picked from a list by the King. It was a largely ceremonial office and although by law somebody from the sheriff's office had to be present at executions, it was most unusual for a sheriff himself actually to take up the opportunity. Invariably in my experience they handed the job down to the under-sheriff, a full-time professional official.

'Bit odd, isn't it?' I asked.

He shrugged. 'Perhaps he wants to see what it's like.'

'We'll have to make it a good one.'

We went down to the execution chamber very early, before eight o'clock, to complete the preparations. There was no need to be quiet; a screw said he was not in his cell. I assumed they had taken him down to the chapel or the exercise yard. The fact that he was not there did not actually make any difference; the habit of working almost silently in this place at this time was so ingrained that we performed our duties in precisely the normal way. We recovered the sandbag which had been stretching the rope overnight; that was spirited away by one of the screws. The sacking on the trapdoor rings meant that there was not a sound as we hauled the doors back up and made them secure.

Within a matter of minutes we were back in our quarters where breakfast was waiting for us – bacon and eggs, always bacon and eggs, and this morning a right greasy mess it was too. I had the butterflies fluttering around in my stomach and ate little. Nothing appeared to bother Pierrepoint and he got stuck in, chomping away, and when he'd finished, wiping his knife on the tablecloth! It was a curious habit that he had.

The waiting was always the worst, but today as the clock moved on my stomach settled and I felt sharp and alert when they came for us. Which was just as well, in view of what happened next!

We walked into the condemned cell on the stroke of the hour. As we entered, Inglis turned round and looked at us. Then he started to smile! At first it was little more than the twitch of his mouth muscles, but blossoming quickly into a full smile as if he were pleased to see us!

As if that was not enough, he then turned his back on us and brought his arms up behind him, hands crossed. He was trying to assist us! As we reached him, I gently took hold of his right arm and raised it slightly. He was being so bloody helpful, he was getting in the way! An instant later Pierrepoint was ready for the arm and I lowered it into his grip.

Without any prompting from me, Inglis now turned and saw the rope waiting for him through the double doors. He smiled again and started towards it. He was about to lead us into the execution chamber!

It must have been a hell of a shock for Pierrepoint. He recovered and managed to get in front, but as he shot past, Inglis speeded up. The man was almost treading on Pierrepoint's heels in his anxiety to get on to the gallows. Pierrepoint looked over his shoulder and started trotting. The two screws who were there to help us fell behind as I hurried after them!

We literally trotted into the execution chamber. Pierrepoint was trotting to stay ahead of Inglis, he was trotting to get there as quickly as he could, and I was trotting to keep up with everybody! As we arrived on the drop I just had time to register the open-mouthed astonishment of someone in the official party before I bent down to strap the legs. Then Inglis was away on that long, eight-foot drop, before I had properly stood up again.

The whole thing had been quite incredible, so fast it was unbelievable. I was down in the pit a few moments later as the doctor checked the corpse, when I heard someone up aloft saying, with disbelief in his voice, 'Seven seconds! It took seven seconds!'

Even Pierrepoint was amazed by what had happened – and

remember that he had experience of more than 600 executions to compare this one with. Back in our room he picked up his cigar. 'By God,' he said, 'by God, that was a quick one!'

'He ran at the gallows', I chipped in, 'and did you see that he smiled when he saw the noose?'

Pierrepoint nodded.

'Have you ever seen anything like it?' I asked.

'No,' he replied. 'I wouldn't mind betting that's the quickest one there's ever been.'

'The High Sheriff will think it was hardly worth his while to come!' I joked.

Pierrepoint laughed.

'Did you see their faces?'

'Bugger them,' he grinned. 'I wonder what my face looked like! I thought, "Christ, the bugger's chasing me!" '

We heard later that it was a record time for an execution in Manchester and I feel sure that it must be the fastest time for a hanging anywhere; I just do not see how it could possibly be done any more quickly, whatever the circumstances.

Thinking about it later – and it was such a bizarre experience that it was impossible to rid it from my thoughts for several days – it was quite obvious that Inglis, as he had said in the courtroom, really did want to be hanged as quickly as possible. He must have asked the screws who were with him what would happen; one of them must have said that he would have his arms fastened behind his back, which is why he had turned away from us and brought his arms up. They would certainly have told him that if he had to go, the quicker he went the easier it would be. It was the old advice that any condemned man got if he asked. The only difference this time was that this condemned man had taken it literally and, as a result, it had all been over and done with in those seven extraordinary seconds.

14 Lovers, an Invitation to a New Year's Eve Party, and More Innocent Men

In the summer I went back to Norwich Prison for the first time since the Goldthorpe shambles. Nothing was said about it but we had a different warder attached to us and I saw no sign of the young chap who had acted as our 'batman' on that occasion. When I found myself on my own with a couple of screws, I asked them how he was and they told me that he had suddenly been transferred to Dartmoor!

The job which took me back to East Anglia was a double: two young labourers who had killed their pregnant sweethearts. There were a number of similarities between the two murders but they were unconnected crimes. It had been decided to hang them together for no other reason than convenience. Dennis Moore was twenty-two; Alfred Reynolds was twenty-four.

Moore was a strangler who had killed his fiancée, a twenty-one-year-old girl called Eileen Cullen, in a cowshed at Catton on the outskirts of Norwich. It was a bizarre affair; they were only two weeks away from their wedding and on the day of the killing they had been out together, first to the doctor where Eileen had been examined to check that her pregnancy was progressing normally, and then they had gone shopping for her wedding outfit. After returning home they went for a walk. There was a row when she would not have sex with him, and he attacked her. Moore himself led detectives to the cowshed and before they could stop him, he ran in and threw himself across the body, crying, 'I love you. I love you.'

Reynolds had shot his girlfriend at Dereham, five days after the Cullen killing. He had wanted to marry nineteen-year-old Ellen Ludkin when he found out she was pregnant, but her father put a stop to any such ideas.

Reynolds was to claim that they had made a suicide pact, and he gave a heart-wrenching account of their last meeting. He went round to her house when her father was out and they had walked to a cycle shed. There he told her that he was going to shoot himself. She said, 'Shoot me first – you can't leave me in this world all alone. Let's go together.'

Reynolds loaded the gun and pointed it at his head but she pulled the gun down to point at her own face and said, 'Shoot me first.'

They stood looking at each other and then she said, 'Goodbye darling. Keep your promise,' and pulled the trigger.

It was heart-breaking stuff … but there were one or two problems with his tragic tale, even apart from the fact that he had a gun and cartridges with him when he went to see Ellen. First, as the prosecution was quick to point out, the distance between the end of the gun and the trigger was too great for the girl to have fired the weapon. Secondly, for a suicide pact it had not gone terribly well – he was still very much alive! Reynolds explained this by saying that he had put another cartridge in the gun for himself but he did not shoot at once because he wanted people to know why they had done it. Not an impressive explanation, I thought!

When he was charged with murder by the police, Reynolds replied, 'I want to go with her now. I don't want to wait.' By the time the trial arrived he'd had time to think things over and had decided that he did want to wait. In fact he did not want to go at all. The jury took just forty minutes to decide that he was to have no choice in the matter.

I was engaged in respect of Moore. Pierrepoint was the number one and the other two assistants were the Manchester Harry Allen and Les Stewart, now helping at his first execution. Interestingly both Allen and Stewart went on to become number ones when Pierrepoint retired and these two carried out the last executions in Britain, in 1964, when they simultaneously hanged two murderers at Liverpool and Manchester prisons. We despatched Moore and Reynolds without any problems. It was a completely unremarkable execution, about which I was extremely thankful, as no doubt were the prison authorities at Norwich.

I was offered another couple of jobs in the autumn, but both men were reprieved, and then with the year drawing to a close, I had a letter from Birmingham Prison inviting me to assist at an execution on New Year's Day. The arrangements were to be exactly as normal; we would have to report to the gaol the day before, so it would mean we would spend New Year's Eve in the prison. We did not make a great thing of the occasion at home – a sherry at midnight was usually the most that we did – so I had no hesitation in accepting the job of helping to hang Horace Carter.

I have, I hope, made it clear at various points in this story that the execution of condemned criminals was carried out in a cool, clinical way with no emotion ever shown towards the men, however heinous the crime. It was drummed into me from the very start and applied to all my colleagues, prison officials, screws on condemned cell duty – almost everyone involved in the whole judicial process. Detectives could from time to time speak bluntly to us about some particular crime but even that was rare. There was in my experience only one exception to the rules – Horace Carter, who had been sentenced to hang for the sex killing of an eleven-year-old schoolgirl.

Sheila Attwood lived in Caversham Road at Kingstanding in Birmingham, the same street as Carter, a thirty-year-old labourer. Early one evening he lured her into his house with sweets, took her upstairs to his bedroom where he raped her and then, frightened of what would happen when she revealed what he had done, he killed her. It was a messy, botched affair and the little girl died slowly and agonizingly, a fact which was apparent even from the labourer's confession:

> 'I kneeled on her arms and then whipped the pillow from under her head and shoved it over her face. She struggled for a bit, so to finish her more quickly I shoved my fingers round her throat. After that she stopped struggling but she was still breathing so I decided to use string. Either I was weak or did not like doing it or she was tougher than I thought … she was still breathing. I got some cloth and my handkerchief … tied it round her mouth and nostrils … and turned her face down on the bed. There she died.'

Carter waited until dark and carried the child's body out of the house, dumping it in a corporation yard at the bottom of his garden, where it was discovered by a neighbour the next morning.

After his arrest, Carter told the police, 'I am extremely sorry for what I did and ought to get topped.'

It would have been difficult if not impossible to find anyone in Birmingham who would argue with that. Never did Pierrepoint and I get a warmer welcome at the police club in Steelhouse Lane when we arrived before the job ... I lost count of the number of people who wanted to shake my hand and told me how pleased they were to see me.

One of the detectives who had been working on the case told me, 'If ever there was a bugger who deserved hanging, it's him!'

'Get the bastard done quick,' chipped in another.

Feelings were running very high about Sheila's murder, and they also gave me a copy of a sheet which was being circulated from the coroner's office:

* * * *

New Year's Eve

Know ye that on Monday 31.12.51 a special session will be held at the Coroner's Court, Newton Street, commencing at 11 p.m. Carefully selected items have been chosen for this occasion and all are requested to book early.

Carols will be rendered by the departed spirits of the Old Year.

'A Stitch in Time' will be sung by the Mortuary men with a solo of 'I'll Dismember You' given by the pathologists.

'Oh Death Where is Thy Sting?' will be the item rendered by the Coroner's Staff Male Voice Choir headed by John Wilson Leitch.

The Court is refrigerated and air-conditioned and on this occasion smoking will be permitted.

A wide choice of Verdicts will be offered to Jurymen and a tastefully decorated Inquisition will be presented to each serving member upon completion of service.

At the conclusion of the ceremony an urn of ashes will be raffled in aid of the proceedings.

Precordial stimulants will be dispensed at intervals throughout.

Tickets 2/6d. Applications in writing only as there are a limited amount of tickets only.

Following these proceedings the audience will be taken by
specially chartered helicopters to Winson Green where various
items will be executed. 'I'll Let the Whole Thing Drop' by
Horace Carter accompanied by Topham Pierrepoint on the
strings.

* * * *

Carter was the only child sex killer that I ever helped to hang
and I never came across another case where there was such
hostility. Here was a man who deserved all that was coming to
him. I have no doubt that similar thoughts existed inside the
prison, and not only on the warders' side of the bars, but here
whatever feelings there were about Carter were not allowed to
show.

We had a look at him before we went to work to prepare the
gallows and then we settled down to our evening, our New
Year's Eve. There was no extra beer that night, no difference to
the normal routine, and we turned in just after ten o'clock. In
the morning I shook hands with Pierrepoint and the screw who
was with us and there were quiet and restrained remarks of
'Happy New Year' but that was it. We hanged Carter at nine
o'clock. The execution was not timed but it was the usual eight-
or nine-second job. He said nothing to us.

Later we went back to the police club, and there we did start
to enjoy our New Year! The drink flowed even more freely than
usual and not only the beer. A traveller from Babycham had
arrived at the club that morning; hearing that we would be
coming in later he stayed, and liberally handed out his free
samples, so we drank those too! Eventually, a trifle the worse for
wear, I headed off home. My bag felt heavy but it was not until I
got home and opened it that I discovered why – Babycham
glasses, Babycham samples, Babycham ashtrays. The cops had
pinched all his stock and put it in my bag! You can't trust
anyone!

I had another laugh a few weeks later when the income-tax
people asked to see me. I found myself being questioned by a
snooty executive officer, complete with pin-striped suit and
pince-nez glasses. He looked over the top of his glasses and
said, 'We understand, Mr … er … Dernley that you're in private
business.'

'No,' I replied.

'No?' he queried, a mocking sort of smile around his mouth.

'No,' I repeated. 'I don't have a private business. I'm a welder and burner and I work at Sherwood Colliery.'

'But we understand that you also have a private business,' he repeated, the smile gone.

'Well if you know – tell me what the hell it is!' I said to him.

'You have a telephone for business purposes,' said the pin-stripe wonder.

Those bloody telephone people, I thought. As if they had not caused enough trouble! 'Aah, that,' I said. 'Yes, I suppose I have got a business in a way.'

'And what way would that be, Mr Dernley?' he asked, managing to make my name sound like something beneath him.

I looked him full in the eye, smiled, and told him. 'I'm a hangman.'

Oh dear, oh dear! He started, his pince-nez glasses fell off the end of his nose and he only just caught them before they hit the desk. He stammered, 'I beg – beg your pardon?'

Mind you, I was soon laughing on the other side of my face … they made me pay tax on all my fees, every single guinea!

The taxman would no doubt have been most gratified to hear that the next financial year was going to be quite busy … with a double hanging in April and several jobs over the following months! The double execution was at Walton Prison in Liverpool and went ahead amid extraordinary fuss and uproar from people who protested right to the end, and indeed beyond, that we were hanging two innocent boys.

The 'innocent boys' were accused of a dreadful murder in Liverpool. The victim was a reclusive fifty-two-year-old widow called Mrs Alice Rimmer, who lived in a house on Cranborne Road in the Wavertree district of the city. Mrs Rimmer did not go out to work and – echoes of Old Gossy – the story went around that her husband had left her money and she kept it all hidden in the house. Quite late one evening Mrs Rimmer let herself into her house through the front door and was immediately confronted by raiders who were already inside. She was savagely beaten, suffering more than a dozen head injuries, and left critically injured. It took her a long time to die – several hours – but none of the people living around had heard anything and no-one went to the house until the following evening when her son called. Getting no reply, he peered through the letterbox and saw her body lying in a pool of blood where she had fallen, still wearing her coat, and with a bunch of flowers that she had taken home with her, on the floor near her body.

The murder investigation led eventually to two Manchester hoodlums called Edward Devlin and Alfred Burns. Devlin was twenty-two, Burns just twenty-one. They denied any knowledge of the Rimmer killing and maintained that on the night of the crime they had been doing a factory job in Manchester with a third man, a claim which the man, a burglar, backed up.

Devlin and Burns, despite their youth, were hardened villains with long criminal histories. They revelled in reputations as tough men and behaved with astonishing conceit and arrogance throughout the early part of the judicial proceedings, laughing and joking together in the dock, doing their best to irritate police and prison officers, and acting as if they could not care less. The trial aroused enormous interest; the public gallery was packed for every one of the ten days that it lasted, with crowds of people locked out because there was not room for them. On the last day queues started to form outside the court at seven o'clock in the morning and hundreds of people waited outside the court all day for the verdict.

As for Devlin and Burns, they did not even allow the guilty verdict to spoil their image. Devlin attacked the judge, accusing him of being prejudiced in his summing up. Burns went for the jury, saying he could not understand how they had reached the verdict and accusing them of being prejudiced. 'At the Appeal Court everything will come out all right,' he told them.

There he was quite wrong. Following the verdict there was frantic legal action but the Court of Appeal rejected the pleas on the men's behalf and refused to hear 'new evidence'. The lawyers then took their case about the new evidence to the Home Secretary, and Sir David Maxwell Fyfe finally appointed a prominent QC, Albert Gerrard, assisted by Chief Superintendent Harold Hawkyard of Scotland Yard, to carry out an inquiry into the case.

As soon as the guilty verdict was returned, I received a letter from Walton Prison, asking me if I would be prepared to assist at the execution of Devlin. The hangings were initially planned for 18th March 1952, but that date was scrapped when the appeals were lodged. The next letter said that a new date, 18th

April, was fixed but a postponement of a week was ordered by the Home Secretary who wished to give Gerrard time to complete his report and for its recommendations to be considered.

In the condemned cells, Devlin and Burns were still trying to play the hard men, heroes of the Manchester and Liverpool gangs. Burns was even planning the revenge he would take when he was freed – as he felt sure he would be – against the people who had testified for the prosecution. He was to prove the tougher of the two; as the pressure mounted Devlin started to crack. Burns was to keep it up to the end – well, almost the end.

With the new execution date, Friday 25th April, only days away, Gerrard delivered his report. Devlin and Burns were guilty; there had been no miscarriage of justice. The Home Secretary decided that the executions should go ahead.

In their letters, and to the people who visited them in prison, Devlin and Burns still protested their innocence and described the trial as an horrific miscarriage of justice. There were many people who felt uneasy about the conviction, including the lawyers involved in the case, and the families and friends of the two men orchestrated a huge campaign in a last-ditch attempt to save them. As the execution day approached there was a ferment of activity, with vigils and protests and demonstrations outside the prison. It was for this cauldron of emotion that I left Mansfield Woodhouse early on the Thursday morning.

I had a rail warrant to take me to Liverpool but I left the train at Manchester to join up with Pierrepoint at The Struggler. I was pleased that I did; he said there was a possibility of trouble outside the prison. He was planning to drive over, but he was worried that his car might be recognized or that they might even have the number, so he had arranged to park it and go the last part of the journey in a taxi. The prison authorities had given him permission for the cab to drive straight inside. I asked him what he thought of all the controversy and Pierrepoint said that friends of his, in the Manchester police, had told him that Devlin and Burns were as guilty as hell.

There was some light relief on the way over to Liverpool when we found ourselves being flagged down by a police car. A young bobby walked over to us and said to Pierrepoint, 'I believe you were exceeding the speed limit. Can I see your driving licence and insurance, sir?'

'Certainly,' responded Pierrepoint and handed the documents over.

The cop opened up the licence, casually glanced at the name inside, did an astonished double-take – and snapped it shut instantly! 'Carry on, Mr Pierrepoint!'

There was no further mention of speeding!

In Liverpool, we put the car out of sight in a yard behind a fish and chip shop which I think was owned by one of his relatives. They gave us a fish and chip lunch and when it was time to go, telephoned for our taxi; the cab turned out to be a wise precaution.

'Strewth!' I exclaimed as we approached the prison. 'Look at this lot!'

The street, for a couple of hundred yards from the gate, was crawling with people.

'If anybody wants to know who we are, tell them we're relatives just visiting,' said Pierrepoint.

I sank deeper into my corner of the car but the driver threaded his way through without incident and no-one took any notice of us. As we reached the gates, they were thrown open and we were inside. Later, when we met Stewart and another assistant whom I had not met before called Smith, we heard that no special arrangements had been made for them. They had been left to their own devices, but fortunately it was not realized who they were and they passed unnoticed and unchallenged through the crowd.

I had never seen an atmosphere like it outside a prison but the events of that afternoon were merely a warm-up for what was to come the following day. We had some reports inside the prison of what was going on and I later read all the newspaper accounts of what happened; fascinating stuff, given that I had never been outside a prison at the time of an execution.

The crowds started to arrive at the prison gates early in the morning and it was estimated that up to a thousand people were milling around as the time for the execution approached. A few minutes before nine a group of about a dozen women, including relatives of Devlin and Burns, knelt on the pavement and began praying. As the hour struck there was complete silence until a woman bawled, 'God have mercy on these innocent boys!'

The newspapers reported that at ten past nine two prison officers came out and put the execution notices in a glass case on the prison door. A small group of Devlin's family were the first to approach the door and read the notices. One of his aunties screamed, 'How could they do it? Why did it have to happen?'

As they went away, the mother of Burns walked up, shrieked, and was led away to a waiting car in a state of collapse. With members of the families gone, the crowds swirled round the gates and there was soon a 150-yard queue of people waiting to view the notices.

The execution did not stop the campaign about Devlin and Burns; their families continued to protest their innocence and vowed to carry on fighting to clear their names, but they were shattered to read in a Sunday newspaper that the pair had in the end confessed on the gallows. That story was raised in the House of Commons where the Home Secretary gave what seemed like an extremely carefully worded written answer: 'The governor of the prison did not make any public announcement in the sense suggested and I am assured that no prison officer made any communication to the press on this subject.'

So what *did* happen inside the prison, and did Devlin and Burns confess?

We were told that despite their reputations as hard men they were not expected to give us any trouble. On the quiet, one of the warders told me that the pair of them had not confessed; they were still protesting their innocence.

In our quarters that night there was inevitably discussion between some of us about whether or not they would crack and want to go to their graves with clear consciences; Pierrepoint, conspicuously, did not offer a view. I realized that if they were going to say anything it would have to be to the priests or the warders; they were not going to get the chance once we went through their doors.

I felt very keyed-up the next morning and it was the last execution where I tried to shave with a cut-throat razor. My hand had a shake, just a slight tremble, and I had a hell of a job getting a clean shave without slashing myself to ribbons! Pierrepoint looked over to me and grinned. 'I should leave that thing at home if I were you, Syd!' he advised.

The screws who brought us breakfast told us that crowds were forming outside the gates and getting bigger by the minute. I listened, but there was no noise penetrating our quarters.

At about the time that those women outside the prison must

have been getting on to their knees, we were taking our positions in the corridor outside the execution suite; the governor outside the execution chamber, Pierrepoint and myself a pace from Devlin's cell door, Smith and Stewart at the cell where Burns was held. We had been given no instructions to slow down or halt the proceedings if either of the men indicated that they wanted to say anything. The signal came.

As we went in, Devlin spun round to face us. The newspaper pictures had shown quite a handsome chap in a hard sort of way, but he did not look hard now and he did not look handsome either. His face and brow were creased with lines, he was as white as a sheet and he was terrified. He did not resist but I breathed a shade more easily as he began walking through behind Pierrepoint. The others were just a fraction slow bringing Burns, nothing serious, but I had time to look round and watch them approaching after I had finished strapping Devlin's legs. Burns had a warder either side of him, just in case, but the couldn't-care-less tough guy no longer existed. He was as white as Devlin and looked just a frightened lad. As Burns walked on to the trap he stared, wide-eyed, at the figure of his friend, face already out of sight under the hood, and with the noose round his neck. I watched as he was prepared, and I listened. The two men did not utter a sound. A moment later Pierrepoint threw the lever over and they had gone. Neither Devlin nor Burns confessed on the gallows … but they did not protest their innocence at the end either …

15   The Sack?

The end of my career as a hangman came unexpectedly and, at the time, mysteriously. I had no idea why they finished me.

The hanging which was to land me in trouble was at Wandsworth; the execution of a murderer in his early twenties who had killed a middle-aged woman in London. In order to put what happened into context, I should perhaps explain one thing: the number of people present when a sentence of death was carried out could vary enormously. There were only two observers who had to be there, the prison governor and a representative of the sheriff's office. In practice the prison engineer, who was responsible for the scaffold, was invariably present and after that there was a host of other people who could sometimes be there: escorting warders, senior prison officials, the parson, the doctor, trainees, and so on. Governors seemed to have wide authority to deal with the situation as they saw fit. At some prisons, like Manchester, the rule was that as few people as possible should be present in the execution chamber during the final moments, and anyone who was not actually needed was instructed to stay clear. Even the escorting warders were under orders to stay out unless the condemned man was creating difficulty. At other prisons the governors took a different view and there were more people present, sometimes a lot more, and sometimes mysterious official guests.

I was rarely introduced to these strangers, although at one execution I did find myself standing next to a guest when we had finished our job; he turned out to be the governor of a Burmese prison who had been invited to watch an English execution.

'What did you think of that?' I asked him.

'It was very good indeed,' he replied, 'but we're almost as quick.'

The conversation was unusual; for the most part observers

were only pale, white faces jammed against the walls and merely glimpsed out of the corner of the eye as we raced on to the trap. By the time I got back up from the pit with the doctor, they had usually disappeared.

The result of the different practices in prisons was that usually I did not know how many people were going to be in and around the execution chamber as we went to work. Frankly it did not seem important; we were busy, they stayed out of the way, and after the first few jobs they became a part of the scenery to which I paid little attention. It was a bad mistake.

The Wandsworth execution went according to the book; we had him down in eight seconds or thereabouts and went back to our room to wait. The next part of the job, recovering the body, was an unpleasant task but it had to be done. The atmosphere at this time was usually workmanlike but relaxed; it was only a body, there was nothing to go wrong and he was not going to hurt anyone. Again the number of people present could vary but there were always at least four of us: the number one, myself, and a couple of screws to help. On this occasion there was also another man. He was not in prison uniform and I could not recall if he had been present earlier at the execution. He was very quiet; in fact I do not think he said anything and seemed to be staying out of our way.

The atmosphere as we went to work that day was bloody awful. Pierrepoint was not particularly talkative and the two screws were a really miserable pair, as tense and grim as it was possible to be. I thought their attitude was ridiculous; as I have said, it was scarcely the most pleasant job in the world but to have people like that around does not help at all.

I was stripping the last items of clothing from the body when it became clear that the dead man was ... shall I say, well-endowed.

'Now that's what I call a magnificent set of vital parts!' I cracked out.

No doubt there are a lot of people who will say that it was a crass and awful remark to make. Certainly it was a very weak joke. All I can say in my own defence is that the atmosphere was so bad that I wanted to say something to break the tension and raise a laugh; it did not. There was no reaction from the screws or Pierrepoint or the stranger.

That was all there was to it ... that was all it took to get yourself fired as a hangman, or at least suspended, for that was, I think, what they had in mind at the time.

Nothing was said to me that morning, or ever; the letters just dried up. Eventually I realized that something had gone wrong and I came to the conclusion that it might have been that remark, but it was to be twenty years later, when Pierrepoint published his autobiography, before I had my confirmation of my suspicions, and even then it was inconclusive. In the book he gave an account of an assistant making a crude remark as they recovered a body and he said that he had blistered the man until he was white in the face and made sure that he never worked with him again. I say it is inconclusive because Pierrepoint did not blister me, white or any other colour; he did not say a word, either then or when we got back to our quarters.

I do not believe that Pierrepoint would, willingly, have shopped me. My view is that either the stranger who was there, obviously an official of some sort, reported the remark to the governor, or, if Pierrepoint did include it in his report, he only did it because the stranger was present. Furthermore, I did work with Pierrepoint again and not long afterwards; I had been engaged for the job before my *faux pas* at Wandsworth and it was obviously decided to let the arrangements stand.

Leslie Green paid for his crime on 23rd December 1952 at Winson Green Prison in Birmingham, less than forty-eight hours before the dawn of Christmas morning. It might seem a harsh decision, to have the gallows operating at that time of peace and goodwill to all men, but though prisons might have their trees and their carol services and even their special dinners, the condemned suite was one corner of the gaol which was never touched by Christmas. The wheels of justice ground on regardless of season or festival, and during my service as a hangman we were almost always called into action in the few days before or after the celebration.

As it happens Leslie Green was something of a special case who deserved no special consideration, at Christmas or any other time. All murders are nasty, brutal and horrible, but even then there are some crimes, perhaps a handful in a decade, which are so evil or wicked or shocking, that they dwarf the others, even in this realm of nightmares. Green had committed such an offence. 'The most vicious murderer of the century' was the way that he was described, and the words came not from some over-excited popular newspaper reporter but from Professor James Webster, one of Britain's most experienced Home Office pathologists; clearly not a man not given to exaggeration.

The professor was speaking after he had examined the body of Alice Wiltshaw, the sixty-two-year-old wife of one of the country's leading pottery manufacturers.

The Wiltshaws lived in a fourteen-roomed mansion on the outskirts of Barlaston in Staffordshire and it was there that they employed Green – a small-time crook with a history of petty thefts and minor offences – as a chauffeur and gardener. Green was with them for two years before getting his marching orders after using one of the cars for his own purposes without permission. That, so far as the Wiltshaws were concerned, was the end of the matter, but Green had not finished with them. Nursing his grievance, aware of how rich they were and what valuables they had in the house, he was determined to get even and this he did with great ferocity late on a summer's afternoon in July.

How far Green intended to go when he raided the house is a matter of speculation. He knew the layout of the house, knew the pattern of the Wiltshaws' lives, when they would be there and when away, so if his intention was merely to relieve them of some of their jewellery and valuables, an experienced thief like him should have been able to do it with no-one harmed. That he might have been planning something more is suggested by his elaborate attempt to get himself an alibi. At lunchtime he was in the bar at the Station Hotel in Stafford, miles away from the Wiltshaw's home; he ate there and certainly did not leave until half past three. He then slipped away, caught a train, did the job, got back and was in the hotel again just three hours later. His efforts though were wasted; Geoffrey Farr, the manager of the hotel saw him come back in and was quite sure that he had not spent the whole afternoon there.

What actually happened at the house was that he attacked Mrs Wiltshaw; a merciless assault which started in the kitchen and continued down a passage and into the hall as the old lady, badly injured and pouring blood, tried desperately to get away from the man who was hurting her. Green hit her with everything he could lay his hands on – a 2½-foot log, vases, ornaments – and finally he dealt the death blows with a three-foot long poker. As she lay dead or dying on the floor, Green finished off his berserk attack, stabbing her in the head with the poker, ramming it up through the chin into the skull again and again.

'In all my experience', a stunned Professor Webster said later, 'I have never come across a case where such brutal and vicious blows have been struck by a murderer.'

The photographs taken by the police scene-of-crime men were so awful that the judge at Green's trial ruled that they could not be shown to the jury. The judge made a sensible decision – our friends in the police made sure that Pierrepoint and I saw the pictures before the job! They really were stomach-churning; the old woman's head was cracked like an eggshell.

At no stage did Green show any remorse or regret. At the hotel, only an hour or so after that dreadful slaughter, he had a drink and a chat with the manager and seemed totally at ease. When he was arrested he denied having killed Mrs Wiltshaw, he denied having stolen any jewellery, he denied having been near the house. At the trial he shrugged his shoulders and said that he was almost indifferent to his fate, whatever it was. After five months in prison he was no longer worried.

His fate, as he knew full well it would be, was to meet us one morning, and we duly hanged him the day before Christmas Eve. He took with him to the grave one secret that the detectives would dearly have loved to know; the place where he had stashed the valuables he had stolen from the Wiltshaws' home. The haul, mainly jewellery, was reckoned to be worth at least £3000; it was an enormous sum of money at the time and only about £250-worth was ever recovered.

To this day I have no idea if the police visited Green in the condemned cell in a last-ditch attempt to persuade him to say where the haul had been hidden. All I can say is that, contrary to the belief of some newsmen, detectives were not at the side of the gallows hoping for a last-minute word before his death; nor were we briefed by the authorities to keep our ears open for anything he might say. At the speed that we hanged him, he would have had the greatest difficulty saying anything at all, even if he had a mind to.

The doors of Winson Green Prison clanged shut behind us at some time around half past ten and we went off to have a post-execution drink with our police friends. As it happens we did have something to celebrate ... for the first time in memory, we had been given a pay rise! My fee had been increased from three guineas to five guineas, still paid half at the time, and half later. News of the pay increase had been announced by the Home Office earlier in the year, without saying what the fees were, and there was a further illustration of just how effective was the secrecy surrounding executions when one national newspaper reported that hangmen's rates of pay varied in different parts of the country. Quite untrue ... and I do not think it had been the case in this century!

As it turned out, the Green execution was the only job where I was paid five guineas. I was never to help hang another man and I was never to set foot in a prison again. Later that day I said cheerio to Pierrepoint and made my way to the station. At no point that morning, or indeed the night before when we had been locked in our quarters together, had he warned me that I was in hot water with the authorities. I never saw him again.

As I said earlier, I think the original idea might have been to leave me out in the cold, but only for a few months ... a sort of suspension. At any rate, there were suddenly no more brown envelopes; executions came and went but there was no call on me. At the time I could not imagine what had gone wrong and why I was so obviously out of favour. I did not believe that it was anything to do with the way that I had performed my duties, I had never been criticized; quite the reverse, I had been praised on many occasions for my quickness. I telephoned Pierrepoint at his pub; he was sympathetic and told me it was just the way things went.

As the months went by I went through a series of emotions; first that of mystification, then concern and finally, much to my own surprise, I found that I was relieved that it was all over. I would not have given it up, but when it had given me up I realized that I'd had enough. Great as my interest in crime and criminals still was, my appetite to be involved had been sated and the novelty had worn off. I also have to admit, being honest, that it was beginning to get to me as well. I think that process had started with the three jobs in two days in London; it was too much and I could not forget the words of that young lass in Mansfield as I went home: 'Did you see that man – what terrible eyes!'

By the middle of the year, I had come to regard myself as an ex-hangman, so it came as quite a surprise when, out of the blue, one of the familiar prison envelopes arrived in the post.

'Dear Sir,
   The above named is in my custody under sentence of death and I have to enquire if you will be available to act in the capacity of assistant executioner when the sentence is carried out?'

The 'above named' was Mrs Rose Loan, a thirty-three-year-old woman from a village in County Durham who had strangled her eight-year-old son. This strange, sad woman had an obsession that she and the boy would be better off dead.

I knew that she would not hang but, a little to my own surprise, I accepted the job. All I can put it down to was the advice drummed into me on numerous occasions by Pierrepoint: never turn a job down.

Mrs Loan was duly reprieved. Ten years later she committed suicide; she hanged herself.

After the Loan case things went quiet for another five months and then in November there was another offer of a job. The letter was from Durham Prison and the execution was that of Charles Hall, a widowed pensioner from Sheffield, who had been sentenced to death for gassing his twenty-four-year-old imbecile son. Again I wrote accepting the engagement but Hall was reprieved a week later.

The year 1953 came to a close with no further prison communications. It meant that I had not been in action for a complete year, but 1954 was only a few days old when I was offered two more executions. The first letter came from Pentonville Prison and concerned a forty-two-year-old man called Zalig Lenchitsky who had killed a five-year-old girl at Bethnal Green in London. Lenchitsky was simple – that much was accepted even by the prosecution – and he had been in and out of institutions and special schools since the age of five. The jury convicted him of murder but added a rider recommending mercy, which was unusual in the case of a child killing. The Home Secretary granted a reprieve.

The second letter was from Wandsworth Prison where they had a twenty-year-old labourer called Michael Davies in the condemned cell. Davies had been sentenced to death for the murder of a seventeen-year-old youth who was stabbed to death in a gang fight on Clapham Common. It looked to me as if there was every possibility that this execution would go ahead and, to say the least, I was concerned that after such a long period of inaction I might be rusty, but on 22nd January I had a letter from Wandsworth; the execution was off, Davies had been reprieved.

That was the last of those cheap brown envelopes I was ever to receive. I was never told I was off the list, let alone why. There was no letter of thanks for my service; merely a silence which has lasted to this day.

16 Conclusions

It is now more than thirty-five-years since I last helped to rig a gallows on the eve of an execution, or felt the butterflies in my stomach as I stood outside the door of a condemned cell on execution morning, or saw a strapped and hooded murderer plunge into eternity. It is now more than a quarter of a century since anyone has seen these things in Britain – more's the pity. Despite the years, it is all as clear as if it had happened only yesterday. I can close my eyes and relive, moment by moment, the very first execution I saw, that of the Hollybush Murderer, James Farrell, back in 1949. I can still see the look of dread in the eyes of Timothy Evans as we entered his cell. I can still hear Norman Goldthorpe on the end of the rope. And how would it be possible, ever, to forget the sight of James Inglis running to meet his death on the gallows.

I have no regrets about what I did and I sleep pretty soundly in my bed. Like most people then, I believed in capital punishment and, like most people now, I still do. The only difference between then and now, I feel, is political will. Members of Parliament in those days were not afraid to be tough. Today they ignore their constituents' views every time there is a vote on the death penalty, and the result is that the country gets wilder and wilder.

I never had any doubts that hanging was a deterrent and I believe it still would be. The atmosphere in a prison at the time of an execution was awesome. Here was a building packed with the rowdiest, most undisciplined, violent men in the country and yet there was not a sound to be heard; the silence was eerie. There was a reason they were so quiet; they all knew what was going to happen and they were frightened. When those great doors went down, sending a boom throughout the prison, they also sent a message, and the message of the gallows went home to the people who needed it most.

That it worked is obvious. Very few of the people who passed through our hands were habitual criminals. The dregs of the criminal world will always go as far as they dare; very few were prepared to risk their own death on the end of a rope. The gallows meant there was restraint; now there is none and we are paying for it. Guns, once the province of the criminal lunatic fringe, are now routinely carried; muggers are prepared to kill for the contents of a man's wallet; there are people on the streets who would snuff out a life with scarcely a thought. Today they are sentenced to life imprisonment and leave the courtroom secure in the knowledge that they will be free again in ten or a dozen years, unless they are very unlucky, and they will live to a ripe old age. What terror it must strike into their hearts!

My blood ran cold quite recently when I read the story of one animal, who had knifed a perfectly innocent man to death in the street in front of his wife and child, standing in the dock at the Old Bailey laughing at the judge as he was sentenced. 'Thank you,' he said. 'Thank you very much!' I never read of anyone laughing when they were sentenced to death.

I have heard it argued that murder is a special crime which is, for the most part, outside the range of normal criminality: people who kill their loved ones, or former loved ones; people who have too much to drink and go too far in temper; people who are suffering from some form of mental illness; sexual perverts who are unable to control themselves, whatever the risks they are taking. These people, I am told, would not be deterred by the gallows. It is obvious that we did not deter everyone, but I am certain beyond the shadow of a doubt that there are some people walking around to this day who would be dead, who would have been murdered, were it not for the threat of the scaffold; I am equally certain that there are others who are prematurely in their graves because the people who took their lives were in no danger of being hanged by the neck until they were dead.

Let me add, unfashionable though it might be, that deterrence is only one factor; punishment is another. I believe in retribution, I believe that criminals should be forced to pay for their crimes, and I believe that killers, who have inflicted pain and terror and death on their victims, deserve to suffer death themselves.

'Wait!' say the abolitionists. 'Mistakes can be made, innocent men could go to the gallows!'

Let us examine this particular suggestion. Let us concede, for the purposes of argument, that every man executed since the war, about whom there is any serious doubt, was innocent. We have Evans, Bentley, Hanratty ... one soon runs out of names.

On the other hand, in the first twenty-two-years after capital punishment was abolished – that is, up to the end of 1987, thirty-seven people were killed by men who had killed before, been convicted of murder or manslaughter, and served terms in prison or special hospital. Now which should be the area of greatest concern?

Before I started to get these memories down on paper it had been a long time since I thumbed through my records ... one brown envelope for each execution; each envelope containing all the newspaper cuttings, the official correspondence and my notes, usually written in the hour between the hanging and the recovery of the body. I found the passing years have made no difference to my views of the people we despatched; I believed then that they deserved to go, and I believe now that they deserved to go – and a lot more besides who were reprieved.

That brings me on to what I believe is the last great mystery about capital punishment: the basis on which the authorities decided which condemned murderers should die and which should be allowed to live. I confess that it baffled me at the time; there was no discernible logic about reprieves. It was not to do with the horror of the crime; some of the killers who escaped the gallows had carried out crimes which were just as gruesome as those committed by the people we did hang. Neither was it a recommendation to mercy from the jury or public petitions which swayed the authorities; they were made in the cases of several of the men that we executed.

Having puzzled away at it, I came to the conclusion that executions were used as deliberate warnings from time to time in specific parts of the country. I do not think the authorities wanted to have many executions but they were prepared to let them go ahead from time to time to make a point; perhaps there had been a lot of criminal unrest in a particular district; perhaps a lot of murders; perhaps a region had not had an execution for a long time. Then a high-level decision was made: let this one take its course.

I realize the theory sounds cranky, but look at the way that I was sent around the country: north-east, London, West Midlands, south, south-west, East Anglia, north-east, north-west. That was only in the first year, and that sort of pattern was to be repeated in subsequent years. I have been able to think of no other explanation for some of the strange decisions that were made.

About executions there is little left to say beyond the fact that I have endeavoured to be as accurate and honest and truthful as I could be, so that the reader should know what it was like on some of the occasions when the most extreme penalty of the law was inflicted. At no point has a deliberate untruth been told; at no point has there been any attempt to hide anything; at no point have I attempted to paint things in such a way that I will be seen in a better light – that, I think, is quite clear!

I hope I have laid to rest the myth that hanging was a barbaric form of capital punishment. The truth is that in the twenty years or so before its abolition in Britain, the system of putting a criminal to death had reached a degree of perfection that I believe is impossible to improve on. The execution was over so quickly that the condemned man could scarcely have registered what was happening to him; certainly he suffered no pain. To this day, I have yet to hear of any other place in the world where criminals are put to death more quickly – and furthermore without spreading blood and guts all over the place. Hanging was a merciful method of despatch.

While we are laying myths to rest, let me deal with another: I have heard it suggested many times that condemned men were stupefied by drink or drugs at the time of their execution. I have seen in a newspaper, the proud boast of the mother of one man who was hanged – he was innocent, naturally – that her son went to his death bravely and soberly, having refused the offer of drink. I have to disabuse her, and anyone else who may believe such things. I never once smelt even the slightest whiff of alcohol when we entered a condemned cell and I never once had the feeling that a man was drunk or stupefied. They all went soberly to their deaths; there was no other way.

The men who operated the gallows were, like the system, the best in the world, and I am proud to count myself in their number. We were, apart from being hangmen, very ordinary people, a ragbag collection of individuals from many walks of life with little in common apart from being reasonably young, reasonably fit and reasonably able to take care of ourselves if the worst came to the worst. Most were family men and most were moderately successful in their lives away from the execution chamber.

I hope it is clear that we were not monsters or hard-hearted or brutal men. There were none who enjoyed killing; such people would have been weeded out by the authorities at a very early stage of the selection process.

Why did we do it? I have tried to explain my own reasons, and for the rest I find it extremely difficult to say because, quite honestly, we never discussed it. That might sound strange – perhaps even unbelievable – but it is the truth. We only talked about our craft amongst ourselves and we were rarely left alone. On a job, from start to finish, we might be unaccompanied by prison personnel for only a few minutes, and we usually had more practical things to worry about than discussing our motives. Once it was all over and we were in a bar or police station, we were usually surrounded by people and it was not possible to talk.

At the end of the day, I suspect there were as many reasons for doing the job as there were men. There were a good number of publicans in our ranks and they all said that being a hangman was good for business! Good for business perhaps, but not I think a reason for doing the job.

Boredom was a factor for some of us, or at least the desire to do something different from the daily grind. It certainly was in my case, although I do not imagine for a moment that modern people, with their cars and travel and foreign holidays, will even begin to comprehend what excitement and adventure those journeys to far-flung parts of the country represented to a young Nottinghamshire pitman. I think my friend, Harry Allen, wanted something different from a life selling ice-creams. Perhaps life could even be dull for pub landlords and bookies!

I have heard it suggested that becoming a hangman was one of the few ways that working-class lads of no extraordinary ability could become famous. It is a wonderful idea and I have no doubt that most of us did enjoy a bit of limelight, even if it was only reflected off Pierrepoint, but the argument misses the point; because of the secrecy surrounding these latter days of hanging, very, very few people knew who we were. There was no fame.

Whatever their reasons for doing the job, my colleagues were, in the main, good men who believed that what they were doing was right, that it had to be done, and that it was for the good of society. I was saddened to hear of the difficulties which afflicted some of them in their later years; several of them had unsuccessful and problematical lives when their hanging days were over.

Kirky, whose brief career as a number one came to an abrupt end after the Goldthorpe disaster at Norwich, became a very strange old man. I went to see him many years later when I happened to be down in his part of the country. He had left the Black Horse and was living alone in a council house after the death of his wife. I did not even recognize the grim man, with large staring eyes, who opened the front door. He seemed pleased enough to see me and we had a cup of tea and chatted about Pierrepoint and some of the jobs we had done together, but there were few glimpses of the old Kirky; this was a different, sadder man.

There was no doubt that he was troubled about his past as an executioner but I could scarcely believe my ears when he told me that the .38 Smith and Wesson revolver he had hanging on the wall was loaded!

'What the hell have you got it loaded for?' I asked him.

'Well, you never know, do you?' he replied, as if that explained everything.

That was the last time that I ever saw him. A few years later I read in the newspapers that he had died.

Steve Wade always did look a haunted man, even when I worked with him on my very first execution. I think he had been on the job for about ten years then and I found him very aloof and withdrawn. He never socialized; he went straight to the prison on the eve of an execution and shot away as soon as the job was over. Ironically, after Kirky had been sacked we exchanged letters and he said that Wade was a man to trust – 'You will never meet a straighter, whiter man than Steve Wade' – but I was never to work with him again and I never did find out if that was so.

My friend Harry Allen, as Pierrepoint told me, gave up because he had been threatened with the sack from his job as an ice-cream salesman, but later he changed his mind and tried to get back on the list. Pierrepoint and I did a job at Birmingham and Harry was waiting for us when we came out of the prison. He got into the car and pleaded with Pierrepoint to get him back in. I was embarrassed to hear it and said almost nothing to him. Pierrepoint promised to see what he could do and Harry got out of the car. As we drove off, Pierrepoint said, 'He'll never do another.'

I never saw or heard of Harry again.

Even the great Pierrepoint developed some strange ideas in the end. I do not think I will ever get over the shock of reading in his autobiography, many years ago, that like the Victorian executioner James Berry before him, he had turned against capital punishment and now believed that none of the executions he had carried out had achieved anything! This from the man who proudly told me that he had done more jobs than any other executioner in English history. I just could not believe it. When you have hanged more than 680 people, it's a hell of a time to find out that you do not believe capital punishment achieves anything!

Finally ... what of Syd Dernley?

With my hanging days behind me, I went back to Sherwood Colliery where I rose to become the foreman welder in charge of fourteen people. I stayed at the pit until the mid-sixties when I left to take on one of the biggest post offices in Mansfield. I ran it until I retired at the age of sixty.

My interest in crime and punishment never flagged over the years and I continued to add to my collection of books, newspaper articles and memorabilia. By the time my period of service for the Crown came to an end, the collection had increased by a legstrap, actually used at an execution, which somehow or other came to be forgotten in my pocket and was brought out of a prison! I also had an armstrap and a rope – that was genuine but it had not been used. It was given to me by Kirky and was one of the spares on the day when he and Pierrepoint hanged all those Americans at Shepton Mallet.

For a time I was the proud owner of the only set of gallows in the country in private hands. They were orignally installed in Cambridge Prison and were among the things auctioned off when the gaol was demolished in 1937. They came eventually into the hands of a Cambridge University professor and we did a swap – I got the gallows and he got various rare books from my crime collection.

Back home I erected the scaffold in the cellar at the post office and after that there was a constant flow of visitors, from policemen to local business chiefs, who wanted to see them. Sadly, I had to get rid of them when we left the post office and moved into a modern bungalow. I sold them to a Nottingham policeman who wanted them to publicize a book he had written. The last I heard, they were at his house but he had got his orders from his wife, and he was having some difficulty finding a new home for them!

I may have been lucky or I may just have been less sensitive than some of my former colleagues, but I do not believe that my career as a hangman has had any ill-effect on me. Not that you ever get away from it so far as people are concerned – once a hangman always a hangman, it seems. Even after all these years I am still pointed out to people and I have a little chuckle to myself when I find somebody in a pub staring at me in that familiar way and I wonder who has been talking to them. Public reaction has always been overwhelmingly favourable; for every person who backs away from me, there are half a dozen who wish to shake me by the hand and buy me a pint. Most people tell me they think I did a good job and it should be brought back. Some no doubt say, 'Cruel sod' when I have turned my back, but that does not bother me.

It has been suggested to me that the reason the job did not have more of an impact on me was that I was only an assistant executioner, that I did not ever actually push the lever. That is true of course; I never acted as the number one on a job, although on every occasion when I travelled to an execution I knew that I might have to do it if something happened to the principal hangman. I have thought much about it and my strongest feelings is one of regret. I would have done it – I wanted to do it – and no doubt the number one position would have fallen to me at some stage had my service not ended when it did. I am certain it would have made no difference. An execution was carried out by a two-man team; the number one had his duties, I had mine, and both were vital in hanging the man. Put crudely, if we had been about a murder rather than a legally ordered execution, we would both have swung for the death. We were equally responsible.

There have been many executioners in history who turned to religion late in their lives when their hanging days were over. Some indeed were pretty strong on it even while they were operating the gallows, but that never happened to me. Not believing in Heaven and Hell, I do not expect to come face to face with any of our clients again, although that is an idea that has fascinated many of my friends over the years. I remember one conversation as we played a hand of dominoes in the back room of a local pub.

'Do you ever think about them?' one asked.

'Aye, I think about them.'

'Do you dream about them?'

'Yes, they're sitting on the end of the bed.'

'Sitting on the end of the bed?'

'Yes, they're sitting on the end of the bed … with their heads on one side! I look at them and go back to sleep again!'

'Syd! You leg-pulling sod!'

In all seriousness, I do sleep pretty soundly in my bed and I have never been troubled with thoughts about the men that we despatched, although I have to come clean and confess that there is one nightmare. In the dream it is execution morning – and I am the condemned man! The cell door opens … two figures come towards me … my arms are strapped … I see the noose in front of me … they start dragging me towards the gallows … I am screaming for it to stop … and I have woken in a cold sweat!

I have had the nightmare twice. The first time they got me as far as the door leading into the execution chamber before I woke up. The second time they actually got me on to the trap. I am hoping that they do not come a third time …

Index

Absalon, SS, 116–19, 126
Allen, Harry (Birmingham – hangman), 11–12, 33–47, 58–69, 96–103, 156, 158–60, 170–1, 197–9
Allen, Harry (Manchester – hangman), 156, 158–60, 175
American Forces, 133–4
Arctic fishing grounds, 163
Ashford, Surrey, 153
Attwood, Sheila, 176–7
Atwell, Ronald, 106–9, 111

Ball, Billy, 112–15
Barlaston, Wilts., 188
Beaconsfield, Bucks., 84–5
Beesley, Julia, 117–22
Beesley, Robert, 118
Bell, Herbert, 164, 167
Belle Vue Park, Manchester, 51–2, 54
Bentley, Derek, 195
Berry, James, 24, 127–8, 199
Bethnal Green, London, 191
Billingham, 116–20
Birmingham, 32, 58, 86–7, 111, 176–7, 198
Birmingham Prison: *see* Winson Green
Black Horse, the, Elton (pub), 49, 198
Brabin Inquiry, 76–7, 82
Brabin, Mr Justice, 76–7, 82

Bradford, 24
Bridgwater, 106–7
Bristol, 93–4, 108–9
Bristol Prison, 108–9
British Empire boxing, 160
Brixton Gaol, 155
Brown, Berresford, 73
Brown, Frederick, 153–5, 159
Brown, Joseph, 153–6, 159
Brunts Grammar School, Mansfield, 17, 19
Bull, the, Mansfield Woodhouse (pub), 112–15
Bullock, John, 93–4
Burma, 185
Burns, Alfred, 180–4

Cambridge Prison, 199
Cambridge University, 199
Campbell, Dilys, 84–5
Canada, 47
Carey (gamekeeper), 21
Carter, Horace, 176–8
Catton, Norfolk, 74
Chertsey, Surrey, 151
Christie, Ethel, 73–4
Christie, Reginald, 71–6, 81–2, 121
Clapham Common, London, 192
Clumber Park, Notts., 19, 21, 23, 30
Coal Board, 112

203

Cocksworth, Det. Insp. James, 169
Colchester, 70
Commons, House of: *see* Parliament
Conservative Government, 76
County Durham, 191
Court of Criminal Appeal, 156, 180
Crooks, Eric, 17
Croom-Johnson, Mr Justice, 86
Crosby, Nicholas Persoulious, 142–4, 147–50
Cullen, Eileen, 174
Cutbush, Derek (poacher), 19–23

Dartmoor Prison, 174
Davies, Michael, 191–2
Davies, Tom, 117
Davey (farmer), 107
Daws, Det. Supt. 'Whack', 157, 160–1
Dawson, Bill, 110
Derby, Wilf, 112–15
Dereham, Norfolk, 174
Dernley family, 13
Dernley, Joyce, 22, 25–7, 96, 104, 109, 112, 142
Dernley, William, 13–19
Devlin, Edward, 180–4
Dickinson, George, 32–47, 57–8
Doncaster, 58, 148
Durham, 126
Durham Assizes, 121–2
Durham Prison, 56–7, 59–69, 78, 121–6, 191

Eady, Muriel, 74
East Acton, London, 72
East Anglia, 174
Eddershaw, Bernard, 18–19
Elton, nr. Peterborough, 49, 198
Empire News, the, 156
Euston Station, London, 156

Evans, Beryl, 70–7
Evans, Geraldine, 70–5, 77
Evans, Timothy John, 70–82, 86, 193, 195
Exchange & Mart, 24

Fabian, Bob (detective), 156–7
Farr, Geoffrey, 188
Farrell, James, 11–12, 48, 50–1, 63, 193
Finnegan, Barney, 103, 156
Fisher, Albert, 112–15
Folkestone, 96, 104, 108
Foreign Legion, 166
Fuerst, Ruth, 74
Fyfe, Sir Maxwell (Home Sec.), 75, 180

George Cross, 104
Germany, 57
Gerrard, Albert, QC, 180–1
Glasgow, 131
Goldthorpe, Norman, 129–31, 133, 136–8, 140–2, 174, 193, 198
Goodale, Robert, 127–8
Gorman, Mr Justice, 163
Gosling, Frederick, 151–4, 179
Gower, Zbigniew, 93–7, 101–4, 106, 108
Gray, Amy, 164, 167–9
Gray and Company, 116
Great Eastern, the (pub), 129–30
Green, Leslie, 187–90
Gun Club, Mansfield, 18, 21, 30

Hall, Charles, 191
Hallett, Mr Justice, 122
Hanratty, James, 195
Hawkyard, Chief Supt. Harold, 180
Heald, Sir Lionel (Attorney General), 74–5

Help the Poor Struggler, Hollinwood (pub), 49, 51–4, 58, 144–8, 181

Henderson, John Scott, 75–6

Hessle, 164

Higgins, E., 55

Hilbery, Mr Justice, 130

Hinchcliffe, G.R. (barrister), 122

Hollinwood, nr. Manchester, 49, 52

Holloway Prison, London, 55–6

Hollybush Murderer: see Farrell, James

Holmfirth, Yorkshire, 132

Holt. J., 26

Home Office, 74, 96, 190

Home Secretary, 74, 75, 77, 180–1, 183, 191

Horse and Jockey, the, Bridgwater (pub), 107

House of Commons: see Parliament

Howe, Emma, 129–30

Hughes, Mr (hangmen's trainer), 32–47, 56, 65

Hull, 163–70

Hull Daily Mail, the, 169

Hull Prison, 170

Humber, River, 163

Humberside, 164

Hyde Park, London, 36

India, 116

Inglis, James, 163–73, 193

Ipswich, 70

Jennings, Chief Insp., 72

Kelly, George, 87

Kensington Cemetery, 74

King George VI, 48, 95, 171

Kingstone Assizes, 154–5

Kirk, Harry, 11–12, 49–51, 59–68, 96–106, 131–42, 171, 198–9

Klagenfurt, Austria, 55

Kramer, Joseph, 147

Labour Government, 76

Lawrence, Chief Const. Sydney, 168

Leeds, 143, 170

Leeds Assizes, 163

Leitch, John Wilson, 177

Lenchitsky, Zalig, 191

Lilliman, Reg, 16

Lincoln Prison, 26–30, 45

Lincolnshire, 32, 169

Liverpool, 86–7, 179–84

Liverpool Prison: see Walton

Lloyds Bank, Bristol, 93

Loan, Rose, 191

Lofty (poacher), 23–4, 105

London, 70–2, 96–7, 106, 125, 151, 156–7, 185

Ludkin, Ellen, 174

Lyons, Jimmy, 112

MacLennon, Hectorina, 74

Maksimowski, Piotr, 84–92

Maloney, Kathleen, 74

Manchester, 32, 47, 52, 54, 144–8, 156, 158, 170, 180–1

Manchester Prison, 142–3, 147–8, 174, 185

Mansfield, 51, 162, 190, 199

Mansfield Woodhouse, 13, 16, 22, 69, 96, 109, 181

Marwood, William, 127

Massey, Miriam, 143

Massey, Ruth, 143

memorandum of conditions for assistant executioners, 59

Merthyr Tydfil, Wales, 70–1

Moore, Dennis, 174–5

Morgan, Alice, 164–70

Myers, Marguerite, 129

Nazi war criminals, 51, 57
Nelson, Rita, 74
News of the World, the, 25, 49, 105
Norfolk, 129, 137
Norfolk Assizes, 130
Normanton Inn, Sherwood Forest, 21
Norwich, 127–8, 131–2, 142, 174–5, 198
Norwich Castle, 127–8
Norwich Prison, 132–41, 174–5
Nottingham, 199
Notting Hill, London, 72
Nuremberg, 133

Official Secrets Act, 32,111
Old Bailey, 55, 73, 194
Old Gossy: *see* Gosling, Frederick
Oldham, 52
Oliver, Mr Justice, 108
Ossett, 129
Owen, Mr, 16

Palmer, Lily, 106–7
Paragon Station, Hull, 165
Parker, Mr Justice, 155
Parliament, 25, 75–7, 183, 193
Paton-Walsh, Brig. E.R., 26–30, 45
Pentonville Prison, London, 31–47, 57, 70, 73, 75–81, 151, 191
Phillips, Det. Supt. Melbourne, 94
Picture Post, 160
Pierrepoint, Albert, 11–12, 36, 47, 49–54, 56–8, 63, 70, 73, 76–82, 87–92, 95–103, 108–9, 113, 123, 131–3, 136, 138, 140, 142–50, 156–61, 170–3, 175, 177–8, 181–4, 186–7, 190, 197–9
Pierrepoint, Anne, 52, 146–50

poaching, 19–24, 29–30, 105
Pollard, William, 32–47
Portland, Duchess of, 14
Portland, Fifth Duke of, 14–15
Portland, Sixth Duke of, 12, 14, 30
Post Office, 112
Price, Dr David (pathologist), 119
Prison Commission, 25–6, 30, 48, 50–1, 55, 57, 111–12
Probert, Agnes, 72

Queen Elizabeth II, 77
Queens Head, the, Hull (pub), 166

Redel, Roman, 93–8, 101–8
Reid Jock, 51, 109–11
Reynolds, Alfred, 174–5
Rillington Place, London, 70–4, 81
Rimmer, Alice, 179
Roberts, Alice, 155
Robin Hood, 19
Rowe, Les, 114
Rowell, Det. Chief Insp. John, 119, 121–2

St Edmund's Church, Mansfield, 22
Salvation Army, 169
Scarborough, 22
Scotland, 131, 165–6
Scotland Yard, 157, 161, 75–6
Scott Henderson report, 75–6
Scott, N. (solicitor), 121–2
Sheffield, 58, 69
Shepherd, Herbert K.C., 122
Shepton Mallet, Som., 133, 199
Sherwood Colliery, Notts., 17, 24, 179, 199
Sherwood Forest, 13, 19
Short, Hannah, 166

Smith, Charles, 166–7
Smith, Edward, 153–6, 159
Smith (hangman), 182, 184
Smith, Harry, 148, 150
Solomans, Jack, 160
Somerset, 106–8
Soskice, Sir Frank, 76
South Africa, 116
South Shields, 56
Station Hotel, Stafford, 188
Stewart, Leslie, 148, 150, 175, 182, 184
Stockton, 116–17
Sunday Despatch, the, 159
Swansea Prison, 47

Taylor, Bob, 94, 104
Thomas, Harry, 168
Thompson, Reuben, 16, 27
Thompson, Violet, 16
Thoresby, Notts., 19
Trivoli Cinema, Mansfield Woodhouse, 22
Torpichen, Scotland, 56
Turnage, Patrick, 116–25

Union Jack Club, London, 33, 36

Victoria Hotel, Stockton, 117
Victoria Vaults, Hull, 166
Virrels, James, 155–6, 161

Wade, Steve, 57–69, 123–5, 131, 198
Wales, 72
Walker, John, 118

Wall, Ronald, 93
Wallace, Edgar, 13
Walton Prison, Liverpool, 175, 179–84
Wandsworth Prison, London, 37, 151, 155–61, 185–7, 191–2
Ward, Beatrice, 166
Warwick Assizes, 86
Waterloo Station, London, 103
Watts Waters, Dr, 168
Webster, James (pathologist), 188–9
Welbeck Abbey, Notts., 13–15, 19, 23, 30
Wells Assizes, Som., 107
West Hartlepool, 116
Williams, Margaret, 55–6
Williams, Sgt.-Maj. Montague, 55
Wilson, Harold, 76
Wiltshaw, Alice, 188–9
Winchester, 96–7, 108
Windsor, 85
Winson Green Prison, Birmingham, 11–12, 49–50, 86–92, 176, 178, 187, 189
Woolwich Arsenal, 32
Worthing, 155

Yarmouth, 128–30
Yorkshire, High Sheriff of, 171, 173
York Street Junior School, Mansfield, 17
Young Vanish Inn, Glapwell, 23

All Pan books are available at your local bookshop or newsagent, or can be ordered direct from the publisher. Indicate the number of copies required and fill in the form below.

Send to: **CS Department, Pan Books Ltd., P.O. Box 40, Basingstoke, Hants.   RG21 2YT.**

or phone: 0256 469551 (Ansaphone), quoting title, author and Credit Card number.

Please enclose a remittance* to the value of the cover price plus: 60p for the first book plus 30p per copy for each additional book ordered to a maximum charge of £2.40 to cover postage and packing.

*Payment may be made in sterling by UK personal cheque, postal order, sterling draft or international money order, made payable to Pan Books Ltd.

Alternatively by Barclaycard/Access:

Card No.

Signature:

Applicable only in the UK and Republic of Ireland.

While every effort is made to keep prices low, it is sometimes necessary to increase prices at short notice. Pan Books reserve the right to show on covers and charge new retail prices which may differ from those advertised in the text or elsewhere.

NAME AND ADDRESS IN BLOCK LETTERS PLEASE:

Name —————————————————————————

Address —————————————————————————

3/87